Turn to Final
A Guide to Modern-Day Spirituality

Dr. Mark Weisman (D.D.)

Aster Press
an imprint of Blue Fortune Enterprises, LLC

TURN TO FINAL
Copyright © 2023 by Mark-Nathaniel Weisman

All rights reserved. Printed in the United States of America. No part of this book may be used or reproduced in any manner whatsoever without written permission except in the case of brief quotations embodied in critical articles or reviews.

Thank you for buying an authorized edition of this book and for complying with copyright laws by not reproducing, scanning or distributing any portion of the contents without written permission.
This story, experiences and words are the author's.

For information contact :
Blue Fortune Enterprises, LLC
Aster Press
P.O. Box 554
Yorktown, VA 23690
http://blue-fortune.com

Cover design by WAM Creates

ISBN: 978-1-948979-82-5
First Edition: May 2023

*This book is dedicated to the many shamans before me who tried to teach
the world a message of hope and peaceful co-existence
before they were silenced.
May your voices now be heard by the peoples of all the lands and
the hope be restored.*

Table of Contents

Foreword	7
Introduction	11
Chapter 1: Welcome To Your Turn To Final	17
Chapter 1 Exercises	53
Chapter 2: The Evolution of the Self	56
Chapter 2 Exercises	77
Chapter 3: Our Emotional Intelligence	83
Chapter 3 Exercises	104
Chapter 4: Spirituality Understanding	108
Chapter 4 Exercises	149
Chapter 5: Prayer, Worship & Magic	151
Chapter 5 Exercises	169
Chapter 6: Interpretations of the Modern Day	173
Chapter 6 Exercises	191
Chapter 7: Where Do We Go From Here?	194
Chapter 7 Exercises	205
Bibliography	210

"Having a dream is only part of what brings us joy, for the true joy in this lifetime is the sharing of our dreams and their meanings, for our dreams are a direct river of knowledge from the spirits and deities"

-Alaska Úlfhéðnar

Foreword

What are we searching for when we educate ourselves in spiritual matters? For many, the answer to this question may be difficult to articulate. It is like asking the question, "why do we hope to fall in love one day?" or "why would you take the time to summit a high mountain?" You are not paid to fall in love or hike tall peaks, so why pursue it? One might say that such pursuits provide transcendental significance in our lives and that explanations are unnecessary. Another might say that having spiritual understanding is culturally significant and is necessary to fulfill longstanding traditions within your family or community. Why are you reading this book?

When individuals feel a desire to pursue something without a clear understanding as to *why* they are doing it we call this a *compulsion*. To be compelled is to "bring about something by the use of force or pressure." What is causing this pressure for spiritual awareness, and why is this pressure seemingly rising throughout western culture? This desire is real and should not be ignored. This pursuit is significant and necessary for our wellbeing. As you read through Turn to Final, you will understand exactly why human beings feel the desire to connect with the spiritual realm both today and throughout all our recorded history.

I had the honor of interviewing Dr. Mark Weisman in the spring of 2021 where we discussed the topic of spirituality and success. I was amazed by the clarity of Mark's explanations and the relevance of his examples. In a matter of an hour, I left the conversation feeling a greater understanding of topics like the proper use of prayer and the role *intent* plays in shaping our emotional states. He answered questions that I have been reflecting on for years in one or two sentences. As I read through "Turn to Final", I realized that "making the complex, simple" is a skill that Mark possesses. This skill when used for the benefit of spiritual knowledge is rare and extraordinarily useful. I consider this book a gift to any reader looking for a comprehensive understanding of all things spiritual.

Dr. Weisman's life and studies are geared entirely toward a complete understanding of the spiritual realm, both within and unbound by the theology of one faith. Have you ever wondered what truths you would uncover if you took the time to live in the mountains, deserts, and bayous seeking advice from shamans, healers, and spiritual mentors? Imagine taking time to study at Christian seminaries and seeking the guidance of Islamic scholars. What would you be like after a life of such dedication? What if you also fell into the darkness of sin and vice, pushing yourself to the brink of suicide? What would that darkness teach you? What mystical truths would you discover? This book is the magnum opus of such a man.

There were moments where I was brought to tears as I read through this text, the most significant when Dr. Weisman provides us with the following illustration:

> *To fully understand the breadth of a deity from the millions of physical beings who have "seen" him/them is to gather hundreds of people around a canyon and have them gaze across it. Each retells their perspective of overlooking the canyon depth. They each see it differently. This is the same way we gaze upon our deity(s). We can choose to stay in our place and continue to see him/them the same way all the time, or we may change our perspective and see them differently. Ultimately, we are still gazing upon the face of infinity.*

Although "Turn to Final" is the reflections of one man, it considers and respects the perspectives of all faiths. This text provides benefits to folks who are just beginning to explore their own beliefs and those who are well-versed in their own spiritual practices. I encourage you to take the time to utilize the exercises in this text. I would even encourage you to read the final chapter first, so you can use these techniques as you comb through the text, using the exercises as a tool to reflect on how Dr. Weisman's lessons compare to your own ideas. You may find that his teachings strengthened or confirmed your beliefs. You may also find that his perspective altered or even eliminated certain perceptions held prior to reading this book.

This book acted very much as a private mentor in my own spiritual life. I feel joy knowing that you are willing to take the time enhance your spiritual life in this way. Thank you, Dr. Weisman, for sharing a lifetime of your experiences and lessons with us!

Brian RJ Goldsack
Businessman
Fall 2022

Introduction

In the vernacular used in the flight industry, the final portion of a flight, or the beginning of the landing sequence, is referred to as the "turn to final", which indicates that an aircraft is approaching a runway in a controlled method, ready to land. In this same method, I would like you, the reader, to consider the contents of this book.

Many have asked me how they can find the elusive understanding of their own spirituality, and to this point I consider them up in the air. I offer the contents of this book as your Turn to Final, a method for getting one's feet back on solid ground. What can one hope to find within this book about modern day spirituality? Hopefully, an understanding of how those with a different belief than our own have come to their understanding, as well as an acceptance for their different interpretation of the spiritual influences they have personally received.

I believe this is what all books about spirituality should produce, and not a one-sided discussion about why one interpretation is "more right" than any other. We'll discuss the evolution of humankind later in this book, as well as the evolution of the underlying psychological capacity; however, I think it would be safe to say that the physical plane of existence offers a diverse interpretation to our spiritual interface.

While this book will cover the result of five decades of study, I hope it will also provide a legitimacy to the individual development of spiritual understandings throughout the millennia before monotheistic religions rose in influence over the world. I hope to demonstrate the reasonings as to why belief in monotheism would come to influence most of the world. Contained within the same text, I hope to demonstrate the differences between theism, at its core, and the enforcement of the associated behavioral manipulation or "practices" that have led to a slaughter of millions of innocent people throughout the millennia.

While I now recognize these core concepts, the understandings presented throughout this book were as eye-opening to me as I hope they will be for you. Let me be clear: I do not wish to "convert you" with this book, nor will I condemn you to hell if you are content with what you currently believe in your heart. Your theology is what you are intrinsically comfortable with, as your personal spirituality should be comforting, and make sense, above all else. It should bring you peace and tranquility and an overwhelming sense to co-exist with fellow physical souls, regardless of their beliefs. My desire within these pages is to present you with ways for you to fully understand whatever theology you want to believe in. The good news here is that there is no wrong answer. You should be absolutely comfortable within your heart, and it should make absolute sense in your mind, regardless of what religious affiliation you choose to associate with.

My hope is that you will come to this book with an open mind and seek to know the truth to secure a path for co-existence throughout the communities in which we live. I hope that this book explains all those nagging questions such as, "why am I here" or "how did we get here"? The overall direction of this book does not exclude any theological belief. It is hopefully an understanding that each of us has a different perspective of the spiritual forces that interact with us on earth. The overall objectives for this book include helping readers recognize their interaction with spiritual entities providing an explanation as to why most spiritual beliefs can find a thread of commonality, and highlighting the fundamental building blocks for peaceful co-existence.

My personal enlightenment comes from my ancestors: the Celtic Norse in Denmark, the same Celts who migrated north and crossed the Elba River into northeastern Germany from northern France before the change of the geological era. It is through an in-depth study of my ancestral cultural beliefs, contrasted against my graduate level studies in theology, that I was finally able to fully embrace their teachings. The personal channeling of spiritual entities revealed to me, an average man, a view and understanding of the multiple layers of existence as well as the importance of learning the needs of each layer. From that point until now, I have discovered a "river of knowledge" by learning to channel the words, understanding, and wisdom from what my ancestors called the Landvætti, which translates to "land spirits." The Landvætti have lifted the veil from my eyes and allowed me to see the world the way it really is and what it has become. They have explained their teachings and ensured I understood the many different facts within this book. The Landvætti have become my spiritual guides and taught me more than I thought possible. Many of the terms in this book come from the beliefs of the Norse/Celtic culture, and they can also be applied to every form of spirituality up to the current day.

There are two major threads woven throughout the chapters of this book. The first is that there is a spiritual influence that will adjust our base intelligence of the world around us (our psychology), whether we choose to recognize that spiritual source or not. In reality, we are spiritual entities experiencing a physical life in hopes of expanding our emotional intellect, and the only way we can do that is by using this physical body. These emotional alterations to our base psychology give us a better perspective to provide empathy, which is the goal.

Second, by having a better grasp of the spiritual influences within our underlying beliefs, we can be more harmonious with others, thereby encouraging a society structured around our commonalities in lieu of our differences. Having a clear picture about how our emotions drive us with other factors gives us the necessary understanding to seek peace with our physical plane classmates. At its very core, the spiritual realm is based on a system of interactivity. Spirits rely on their empathy for our mental states to establish and maintain a communications channel with us.

Whether we decide to alter our life's trajectory based on the information presented within the text of this book or not is completely up to each individual who reads this. I simply offer the knowledge and wisdom that I've been given by the Landvætti throughout the last five decades, hoping that more people can find this common ground so that we can all come together, eliminating the perceived necessity of excluding anyone because of some beliefs or theology.

Finally, this book will speak about many of these interactions at a detailed level. In the same way, I hope to enlighten you from a scientific perspective about how our plane of existence came to be. In our quest to understand the inner workings of spirituality in our modern day lives, we'll spend some time discussing the science of our theology. Our first step is to understand how everything in existence came to be, and just as importantly, why they have come to be.

Turn to Final

A Guide to Modern-Day Spirituality

Chapter One

Welcome To Your Turn to Final

Our spirituality influences our everyday lives, as well as what we think we know. Whether we subscribe to a religious practice or not is irrelevant. There are spiritual entities who inhabit this plane of existence with us who can alter our most basic thoughts. This fact should cause a moment of pause. If nothing else, consider that seriously and take time to consider the impact of spirituality on both our intrinsic intelligence and ultimately our behavior within society.

This book is not aimed at converting you to any theology other than what you currently feel drawn to. The hope is to convey the realities of life around you and help you to focus on being a better practitioner to whatever you choose to subscribe to. Hopefully, I will provide you with an understanding as to the astonishing uniqueness that you are, and therefore are a part of an incredibly unique relationship with an entity we call a deity. This deity has created an existence cycle that has repeated for millions of years, covering all forms of life from the smallest of cellular level to the ancient dinosaurs of the past. Our deity/

deities) are infinite beings capable of amazing things. In the words written by Rich Mullins in his 1988 album "Winds of Heaven, Stuff of Earth" he quotes:

"Our God is an Awesome God."

I feel compelled by my gods and the spiritual entities I communicate with every day to pass along their wisdom to you, the reader. What you decide to do with this information is completely up to you. Hopefully I will give you some "food for thought" to help us find commonality among all our beliefs so we can begin the process of healing wounds and moving forward with a similar understanding to co-exist peacefully.

In my opinion, the general population's idea of spirituality has faded in the annals of history, although we know its effect on human existence has been monumental throughout the evolutionary process. It has been said that we (humans) need our "religion" neat. We need it to be majestic and regal in nature. I somewhat disagree. While religion may need tidiness, I believe that spirituality exists in chaos. Within this chaos, we find clarity of understanding, and in most cases, the chaos settles following the arrival of our consciousness connecting to our spirituality. This is where we find peace.

We must become open to communications and wisdom from our deities and those spiritual entities who want to help us succeed.

Regardless of your professed religion, or religious practice, there are pieces of knowledge and wisdom in this book that may apply to your life. Most of us have sought an understanding of our existence and have diligently searched for answers to underlying questions. Even if our heart is full within our current practice, we must reconcile within our minds the reasons we believe what we do. In addition, there are many interactivities within our physical lifetime that cause us to question even our most devout beliefs.

Without further ado, let us slowly tilt the control column of our life as we make our "turn to final".

The Path We Travel

Between the time we are conceived until we pass from our physical body, we will have many different challenges and experiences that can define who we are and what we will become. Each step within our lifetime is but a single footprint on the overall path of our existence. Hopefully, you have opened this book with hope and optimism as to what your future may hold, although I must admit that neither I, nor any deity level entity, can possibly know where your path will carry you. By using your free will, you can change your trajectory at any point, for whatever reason you see fit. Therefore, you alone are the motivating force to bring about changes, and to navigate these changes, within your life. By understanding the influences and accepting the ramifications of your decisions, you can successfully navigate your life's trajectory from the beginning to eternity. One needs to always remember in our physical lifetimes that we retain the power over extrinsic influences to change the direction of our lives. While it may be difficult, and the ramifications may enact a heavy cost, we always have the authority to completely alter our life's trajectory and to transform ourselves at the most fundamental level.

At one point in our existence, our spiritual selves consisted of nothing more than a collection of energy particles floating effortlessly in the abyss of nothing. This amassed collection established a consciousness and became self-aware and made the decision to embark upon a physical journey with a physical existence. While most spiritual entities have chosen this path, it is not the only option and therefore not completed by all created spiritual entities. However, for those who decide to take this path, it leads to an education that cannot be obtained in any other way, which is why most spiritual entities choose to be associated with a physical body for an emotional education. The required alterations of sensory input by the chemical influence that we call emotion requires that a biological, physical body be used for this purpose.

Every day, we all have interactions that most of us are completely unaware of. But while most humans are not outwardly religious, we are spiritual beings at our core. It is this core understanding that dictates every facet of our lives. This one fact is what connects us to the natural world around us, as well as to each other, even without our knowledge.

Our physical selves are bound by natural laws that affect every minute detail of our lives. Natural laws like gravity, vacuum, polarity, and time and space, became how we translate everything in an attempt to understand the natural forces of the physical plane of existence. However, our spiritual "selves" are not bound by these same rules, therefore the separation between the spiritual and the biological self becomes that much more important in our discovery of our total selves.

We, as the physical manifestations of a spiritual entity that is confined to our biological bodies for the duration of our physical lifetimes, released following the physical body's demise back to the spiritual realm, are simply travelers through this emotional classroom we call life. Throughout these chapters, I'd like to explain what I have been taught as the spiritual interface with our physical selves. However, I believe that maybe we should back the whole lesson up here a moment and discuss "our path." What are we here on earth to learn, and how is that done?

How Do I Know?

This book is a culmination of over 50 years of study, starting with being introduced to and instructed in the ways of the metaphysical world by my mother at a young age. This led to my journey through every recognized spiritual practice around the world throughout all recorded and unrecorded history, some much more in-depth than others. I spent extended educational tenures in the indigenous practices of the Navajo peoples and learned from the monotheistic practices of Christian and Muslim study and worship, finally arriving at my ancestral Celtic beliefs of the early Indo-European Norse, primarily journeying through the monotheistic practices as an ordained minister, then, after leaving the church, studying and accepting my place as a Celtic Shaman. These studies have gone far beyond the psychological, through the theological, and even beyond the philosophical, to the instinctual thinking of the animal kingdom and our ancestor's ancestors.

Throughout my studies, I followed the development of cognitive thought of the anatomical modern humans (AMH) following the many routes of migration out of Africa. If we take a long look at the parallel spiritual belief development in the many different routes, we find the culmination of similar beliefs throughout the four corners of the newly discovered world without the benefit of direct societal interaction. As we know, any interactivity between cultures would have been extremely limited due to either geographical separation or a language barrier. My further research led to many discoveries about where the spiritual understandings that we all possess were developed from and why these developments became so important. While some of the information here you may have read elsewhere, the solidifying of the information and its application to real "everyday" life has been revealed to me through trances, meditation, or channeling of active spiritual entities, in addition to countless hours of working with hundreds of individuals through many different belief systems as a spiritual counselor for (predominantly) returning veterans of foreign conflict.

While I will not accept credit for the information provided here as it was passed to me from these spiritual entities, I do hope that you find as much value in the information as I do. There are those among us who have yet to move past their practice of obedience to discover the theology beneath the daily rote exercises and still directly associate the theology to its publicly enforced practice. This text is for those who have arrived beyond, or have moved outside their practice, with an honest quest of their core theological understandings.

I am a third generation Celtic Dane born in the United States. My parents were also born in America. My father's grandfather was a northwestern German with lines that trace back into the eastern parts of Germany. My paternal great-grandmother, with her lineage extending over 900 years into northern Denmark, pretty much secures my ancestral heritage to those renown travelers who became known as "the Vikings" before the end of the first millennia. This ancestral heritage provided an underlying need to understand my birthright as a Germanic tribal Dane. This birthright included a trail of what was then called Seidr magic, meaning that my ancestors understood and worked with the same Landvætti that I have come to know and respect (more about magic in a later chapter).

My journey to these beliefs, like most Americans, is rooted in the study and practice of the Christian faith. Along this journey, I discovered my personal heritage and the spiritual worship of the Celtic peoples, which would later become the Norse of myth and legend.

Finding My Way

Although I go into more detail about my life in a later chapter, I'll share a short bit here to provide context as to how I got to this place in the Universe. At a young age I was introduced to the "Universal Energies" view of spirituality from the New Age form of understanding from my mother. Years later, my trajectory intersected with a Navajo medicine man who helped me understand the connections between the physical and spiritual realms and taught me to listen with my heart instead of my ears. This was further revealed during a near-death experience after overdosing during an unsuccessful self-destruct sequence that would immediately move me to an extremely different reality. This new reality introduced me to the most beautiful person in the world: my wife. Her steadfast belief in the monotheistic practice persuaded me to seek guidance through monotheism, which led me to obtaining my undergraduate degree from a Baptist University and becoming ordained in the Christian theology. Next, still not finding an answer of comfort, seeking out the Nation of Islam, then finally, venturing off that path to discover my true beliefs of my ancestors.

I am now home. I have arrived at the Celtic/Norse beliefs of my ancestors of Northern Denmark. I have come to understand that the recognition of my deities by different names was significant, as I've now learned about these infinite beings. The fact that my heart kept asking questions is ultimately the lesson to learn.

I moved further from the practices of the monotheistic churches and found that I began to have nagging thoughts about the many different practices enforced by the church. As I began to investigate these nagging thoughts, "ideas" would occur to me out of nowhere. Later, I developed the understanding and necessity of meditation. I continued to include meditation in my daily life until the winter of 2020, when an event would change me forever.

"That Night" is a recollection of that event in January 2020 that altered my trajectory:

Another overcast and dreary day in South-central Anchorage, Alaska. Overall, the day was spent in modern-day life, and nothing seemed out of the ordinary. Our family (my shield-maiden, my two young sons, and I) celebrated my arrival at 54 years old with a cake and ice cream following dinner. Nothing out of place, nothing unusual about the day at all. It wasn't until we were getting ready for bed that evening that things began to feel "different". I sought answers from my Landvætti, but they were silent. Normally my wife ventures upstairs to bed and I remain downstairs to feed the dogs and put them away (in their kennels for rest). Because she can get energized, my spiritual partner ("Astrid von") sleeps in her kennel in the garage.

Tonight, she doesn't want to go into the garage, even after some strong encouragement, and paws the back door. Without thinking about it, I let her outside again. Her dark coat stands out against the fresh snow in the yard, and I see her bolt for the northeast corner of the property. I shrug it off, thinking she may have seen a squirrel. However, at this point our aged large yellow lab indicates she wants to go outside again as well. Uh, okay. Without thinking, I let her outside again, hooking her collar onto a run (she's blind). As I step outside, I hear Astrid whining. I search for her in the snow and find her laying down in the deep snow in the northeastern corner of the property. Confused, I call her. She stays where she is. My immediate thought is that somehow her collar got caught on something buried in the snow and she's stuck. I decide that I can dash out quickly to unhook her collar and do so.

I don't have any shoes or a shirt on as I run outside. I notice that our aged lab has freed herself of her collar and joined us here in the corner of the property. That's when I heard his voice.

"Oolv heth nar." The deep voice startled me. "Oolv heth nar, do you know me?" I searched the yard through the falling snow to make out anything human. I immediately wondered if I was hearing things. Could the weather have made that sound? Did I actually hear it, or think I heard it? I searched through the darkness that was interrupted only by falling snowflakes. A figure slowly materialized before me, emerging from the darkness. His large frame pressed his cloak in all directions, and fur boots extended from the bottom of his cloak to the ground. He stood about a foot taller than my six-foot height and was wider at the shoulder by a foot in each direction. His face was partially covered by a darkened hood, and his thick beard stuck out, as did his long braid of hair. A large hand grasped a weathered staff. As he got closer, I noticed that the snowflakes did not pass through him but settled on his person. My mind immediately began to contemplate how I could fight my way out of this situation with my dogs. Although my partner Astrid did not move as he approached and allowed him to give her a scratch behind the ears (she normally doesn't like anyone she doesn't know). "Oolv heth nar. You are the great-grandson of Jens Petersen's youngest girl. Are you not?" As he spoke, I mentally tried to remember the ancestry stuff I had completed for my mom recently. "Your father was Albert

the oldest boy, and his father was Albert the oldest boy, and your great grandmother was Nelsina." As he spoke, he lowered his hood, which revealed his aged appearance. Although he seemed quite aged, his hair and facial hair were blond, almost golden, with a braid of hair that ran from the back of his head to reach into his cloak in the front. The single most striking of all his features was the large patch covering the space of his right eye. The patch didn't have any strings and was tightly placed over the eye socket.

My mind was racing to apply some logic to what I was seeing. At this point, a random thought struck me. I was barefoot in 18 inches of fresh snow and had no shirt on, yet I was not cold. Another thought shot through me. "You are Óðinn," I stuttered and immediately dropped to one knee in the fresh snow. He reached out with his free hand and grabbed my arm, lifting me back to my feet with ease.

"You will bow to no one. Ever," he spoke evenly. While there was no real inflection in his voice, there was a tone of finality to it. As if his words were carving law as they traveled. "You have learned much; do you remember us?" As he asked his question, he waved his staff in a general direction, indicating all around. I turned and saw hundreds of human outlines surrounding us. I couldn't discern the details, simply darkened human outlines. Some of them stood where I knew there was a fence, and I could see the fence through their darkened outlines. "You have spoken to the Landvætti many times, and they are sure you are whom I seek." He stepped closer to where I could now plainly see the patch covering his right eye.

His chiseled facial features left an indelible mark on my memories. I will never forget that face.

As he leaned closer, I saw the pelts beneath his cloak as well as the head of an ax upon his chest. "Let me see you. Your great grandmother carried the gift of the Norse magic in her blood, given to her by the elves of Álfheimr." He gave a slight smile. "Yes, I believe you are one." The smile disappeared as he continued. "I came to your father and your grandfather, and they denied me. Instead, they insisted on forging their own paths." He looked off into the distance. "I have been watching you and seeing where your heart is. You have proven your allegiance to me and to the Landvætti." He turned and cast his steel-gray eye on me, as if he was looking through me. "What is your desire? Do you wish to assume your birthright?" Astrid let out a small whimper and when I looked down, she nudged my hand with her nose.

I turned back to the figure who stood before me. "With all my heart, I do. I am the great-grandson of Nelsina Petersen of the Petersen clan and a proud Germanic Dane." Although what I said was absolutely true, I tried to sound more "official" than I felt.

He reached out his right hand, and I grasped his forearm. I felt the leather armor covering the supersized forearms beneath the cloak. The figures surrounding us moved closer. They reached out their arms to lay hands upon my shoulders, and the words came into my mind,

"Almighty all-father in Valhöll, I am before you this eve to swear my unwavering allegiance to you. You know I have proven myself in battle, both in the physical and spiritual realms. Do you remember the time where I crossed the BiFrost to learn of the other realms? Or the time I crossed into the realm of Hel to protect the young girl who was threatened in her dreams? I have proven my faith in your power over the natural world. I have proven my ability to cross the boundary from Miðgarð to the other realms and have negotiated with Heimdal for safe passage. I have drunk from the horn of Kvasir, filled with the mead of Óðrerir and have been granted the infinite wisdom brewed of his blood by the dwarves. I swear upon my honor to be dedicated to you, else accept my fate of drowning in the black river filled with venom between Niflhel and Narstrand. I stand ready to serve you against the forces of ice giants should

they escape Jötunheim. I swear to give my last breath to you in the battle of Ragnorök. Please accept my blood as a token of my oath as I endure the pain of surrendering it, as I swear this oath on the ring of Úllr to verify its honor." I drew my knife from its sheath on the back of my pants (almost feeling obligatory) and drew it across my forearm, so the blood flowed down onto his forearm as well. I felt the sting of the knife blade slicing through the outer layers of my skin, deep enough to create a substantial blood flow; however, I kept my grip firm on his forearm. His stern gaze melted to a smile as he drew the axe from his cloak and slid it across the skin on his forearm, forming a pool of blood between our arms. I remember seeing in my peripheral view the pool of blood mixing and forming shapes of the runes. Óðinn put the axe back into his belt, and dipped a finger into the pool of blood, then reached up and drew the rune Uruz on my forehead.

"We are one," he stated. "The Nornir spoke of this moment." He laughed as he spoke, and he was loud enough that I wondered if we would wake my wife since the window to our bedroom faced where we stood. "They told me that there would be another Úlfhéðnar. That all was not lost," he said, and with that, he released my arm and grabbed both sides of my face, pulling it toward his until our foreheads touched. He spoke more quietly. "The Landvætti will teach you. Listen to them. They are our friends. Learn what you need to know. This is your birthright. Nelsina was right about you. She told us you would rise." He stepped back. "You have sworn an oath to the Úlfhéðnar. In our beliefs, there is no stronger bond in this world than the oath of a man to me. The path that you have chosen to endure will be hard, the young will cast you out, the devout may doubt, but ultimately, the victory will be yours, as you are sworn to uphold the life of the Úlfhéðnar. The Landvætti are at your command to ensure our ways continue."

I felt as if a great weight had been lifted from my chest and energy surged through my body. He turned to go. "Úlfhéðnar, you have made me proud, as well as your ancestors. Today is a day to rejoice, for today our way of life is on its way to life."

A raven appeared and landed on his left shoulder. "You have done well, my friend. You found him." He spoke to the raven without taking his eye off me. "Prepare yourself, Úlfhéðnar. Challenges will come, but you are ready." He turned to leave, then added, "You know in your heart what you must do. The tide is changing. It is time to bring the ways forward." His outline disappeared into the falling snow, and before I could say another word, the figures faded away to reveal the falling snow.

Astrid nudged my hand again. I looked down to see my arm was still bleeding, dripping onto the newly fallen snow. Astrid and Ember led the way back to the door we'd come out of. At this point, I realized my bare feet again. The cold was harsh, and I felt the ache of the cold seeping in. The dogs led the way inside, and I quickly found a paper towel to apply to the wound. I covered it for about a minute when I found it had stopped bleeding. I helped the dogs to bed, then washed my hands, rinsing a substantial amount of blood down the drain. I went to wash my forehead where I was sure he had marked it but found it empty of blood.

When I went to bed that evening, I expected a night of restless sleep, with visions and ideas racing around my mind like it happened every night. Tonight was different. Instead, I floated in a warm lake. I felt a gentle washing over my body. It was, without close comparison, the best rest I ever had — before or since. Ultimate peace and solitude. I felt myself melting into my bed. When I awoke the next morning, it was as if I had turbocharged my batteries.

While the discovery of my true "calling" was quite dramatic, after doing some research, I learned that these types of visions and interactions were quite frequent among our indigenous Native American brothers and sisters and were a legitimate recognition of the "spiritual self" coming to the center of our focus. Since that winter day in early 2020 until now, I have worked fervently with the Landvætti to help others find peace by teaching coping mechanisms with their inability to reconcile the acts of war to the teachings of enforced monotheistic practices of modern society. I've assisted many in understanding the differences between the enforced practices throughout the millennia and the underlying theology to assist people in averting the need for the guilt and shame that accompanies the modern monotheistic practices.

Understanding the pieces of guilt for what they really are: lessons to learn. I have also come to understand that these lessons, once learned, release the original guilt memory to allow our minds to focus on other thoughts and beliefs. I shared this understanding with the many individuals I have worked with, all to free their minds in order to address the larger psychological trauma they had endured.

Understanding Our Path

After becoming self-aware, spiritual sources will seek out a newly conceived biological life form within the physical plane. While there are many different forms of life here on the physical plane, and there are many differences within the education curriculum between each, whether a newly formed spiritual entity choses the animal kingdom or maybe the plant environment, or maybe choose a human physical form, they will complete the lessons given for the particular vessel for learning the need to control the emotional experiences throughout a physical lifetime. Because our spiritual "selves" are not bound by any time constraints of the physical plane, we may choose to visit the physical plane multiple times, each time in a new physical conception, as physical selves are biologically limited to one lifespan.

The path that we travel throughout this lifetime would seem to have two alternate routes. The first path, or "default" path plotted by "the fates" or, some of the "Landvætti" (more about these in a later chapter) would have us experience the emotional minimums to consider the lifetime a success in accomplishing the emotional experiences necessary to move to the spiritual plane. The alternate path is the one we choose. This is where the establishment and understanding of "free will" comes in. As we travel from creation to eternity, we are free to make changes in our experiences along the way, in any way we desire. Knowing that we accept full responsibility for the learning associated with the ramifications of that trajectory change, we are in total control of the journey we take through our physical existence. Most decide on a hybrid of these alternatives, where they make some trajectory changes then switch to the minimum trajectory for a period. This model seems to fit an understanding that many have expressed about "sometimes you eat the bear, sometimes the bear eats you."

In some cases, the educational experiences necessary for a complete education are cut short, thereby terminating the lessons of emotional control. In these cases, some may choose to revisit this plane in another physical conception or inhabit the spiritual realm instead. Either way, the end goal of obtaining some level of emotional understanding, and therefore control, is a highly sought-after ability within the spiritual realm. Throughout our physical lifetimes, we will interface with thousands of other physical entities, all attempting to accomplish the same goal: an achievement of this higher level of emotional intellect. Some of these entities we may discover possess a stronger bond between the selves than others. We'll discuss the idea of "frequency matching" later in the book, but suffice to say, the more closely our personal aura's frequency matches another's aura, the closer we feel toward that individual. A level of trust is established within this aura frequency matching. This is the underlying mechanism that allows us to locate those who are like-minded and who are "friend or foe." It also introduces the spirit to the emotional influence such as love or compassion.

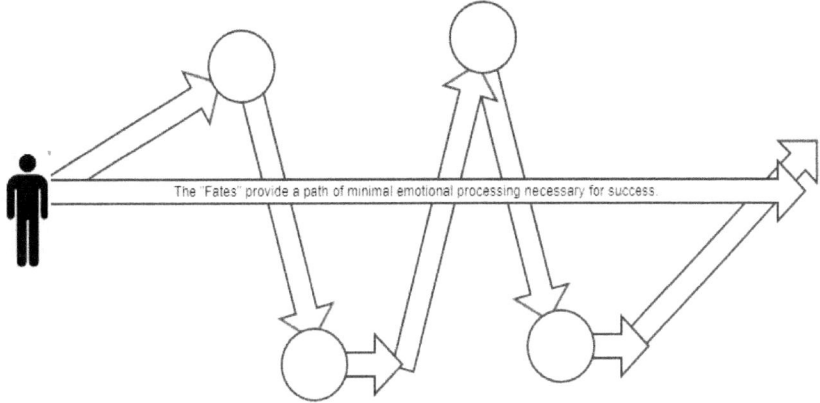

Figure 1 - *The path that is planned for us is typically not the one we take because of the possible desire for emotional controls perceived as necessary.*

The path that we will travel on the physical plane is almost never a straight line, as our spiritual self is pulled or pushed in many directions, sometimes simultaneously. In addition, we may inhibit our own success by utilizing the biological modifications of the intrinsic chemistry with these phenomena called "emotions". Emotions are pivotal in our success here on the physical plane, as their control is our primary life lesson. As we travel our path in the quest for our emotional education, we need to be cognizant of all the entities who are within the scope of communications who can help us navigate the chemical maelstrom that emotions bring into our lives.

My personal path (as an example) has been a twisted train wreck of an educational endeavor, and it is only by using the gift of hindsight that I am able to understand the twists and turns that the Landvætti suggested into my life that has brought me to where I am today. This journey, which has taken over fifty years so far, has been fraught with emotional lessons.

When I was very young, my mother was interested in metaphysical and channeling practices at the time. Her energy focus entered my thought process, and I unknowingly began a journey of understanding and clarity.

While the lessons at this young age offered insight as to the spiritual communications that our physical entities could engage in, these early lessons would incite my desire to further understand.

> *This would be followed by a multi-year tutorage with an indigenous man from the Navajo tribe in Tucson, Arizona, who introduced me to the spiritual world around us. I didn't realize it at the time; however, this was where I would be introduced to (what I would come to know as) the Landvætti. Through meditation and trance work, I was able to communicate with the Landvætti.*

These lessons showed the importance of meditation and taught me to listen with one's heart, to minimize the extrinsic influences. Listening with one's heart generates the inclusion of emotions connecting us to the spiritual realm.

> *When I was about 14 years old, in a heated departure late one evening, my father and I met in the circle of hand-to-hand combat for the honor of our little clan. In a rage, I was able to subdue him and force him to surrender and flee. From that day until now, I always wondered if things would have stacked up differently for my family had that not happened. I now have my answer.*

This experience brought emotional chaos, as my conflict with my father was based on my alignment with my mother's frustration of years spent hostage to emotional blackmail. This is also where I began to learn that although "might was right" that evening, the emotional baggage carried a heavy burden on my young, developing understanding.

> *Toward the end of my three-year tour with the US Marines, I found myself heavily addicted to cocaine and heroin. I relied on these substances to quash the voices in my head and emptiness in my heart. I was discharged and returned to my (then) home in Tucson, Arizona. However, the need to maintain a level of control of the voices remained. Upon my return to Tucson, Óðinn taught me mercy as I became the primary caregiver for my terminally ill*

father until his death a mere forty-five (45) days after.

Following the death of my father, I spent a year living in a tent on the mountainside of the Santa Catalina mountains just north of Tucson, trying to make sense of my life.

The year on the mountain led to a substantial amount of trance work and meditation, which strengthened my spiritual connection to the Landvætti temporarily. I would come to learn the ways of the Landvætti as well as the truth about the channels within each of us that allowed them to communicate with us. However, this time was followed by a three-year destructive period, where I would ultimately not see any way out.

Toward the end of my destructive journey, I lived in a culvert for approximately six months. During my life in the culvert, I survived a near-death scenario caused by a heroin overdose, followed by intervention, or "cleansing" beginning a multi-decade journey without the need for the drugs in my life. This situation was ultimately enlightening and began to clear my eyes of the fog. While I didn't know it, this is where Óðinn reconnected with me. Throughout the following thirty years, Óðinn has raised me from the ashes of who I was and allowed me to discover my true path.

In my beliefs, this self-destruct portion of my life resulted from my misunderstanding of the information I absorbed into my thinking. Between my ego and my self-loathing, I fought substantial internal demons to understand what was being taught.

Following the cleansing, I packed up all my family's estate that had been left in my care into an older model truck and moved into my brother's barn 1,200 miles north on Whidbey Island, Washington.

After being on Whidbey Island for about four months, Óðinn introduced me to my "Shield-Maiden" who would become my wife and the mother of my children. Ultimately, she never gave up on me. Within six weeks of meeting, we were married in a small ceremony in a bar in Mount Vernon, Washington. We have now been together for over thirty-two years.

While she has embraced the monotheistic doctrine leading her to a different journey, she is my world. I cannot begin to form the words of thanks for the belief she had in me. She led me on a path of discovery as to the deity communications that she interpreted as the right path.

This path of monotheism taught me how the deities communicate with us during everyday life. As I learned to listen with my heart, I focused on the interpretations I received. I studied in earnest and began to focus on what seemed to be multiple perspectives provided through my interpretations of what I was understanding. This emboldened my need to understand.

Eight months later, I was honored to meet my daughter, born at the University of Washington medical center in Seattle, Washington. My beautiful, intelligent daughter is now grown up, has married a good man and given me my first grandson. The third generation of mine. I am truly honored.

Although my life seemed to be moving in the right direction, I remained unsettled and continued with my internal battles with Hel, almost ending our newly formed marriage on many occasions. Repeatedly, Óðinn interceded and settled my wife's heart that she would forgive me, again and again.

Several years later, I was introduced to our twin sons. With great stress and concerns, the boys came into this physical world. They are now adults, with one of the boys giving me my first granddaughter and second grandson, while the other chose the warrior's path within the military.

The next gift was the use of Óðinn's gentle hand to guide me to enroll in a Baptist University, where he presented me with an instructor who would be instrumental in reconnecting me to my ancestry. While he may not have known it, my theology course at Wayland completely changed my life's trajectory. Although not immediately, my return path to Óðinn was forged. I would learn about monotheistic beliefs and the psychology behind them, which ultimately led me home.

During my time at Wayland, I became ordained as a Christian minister and tried to reconcile what I felt in my heart with what was being taught. I spent a decade as a chaplain who worked primarily with returning veterans and their families, particularly with symptoms of PTSD. The voices of the Landvætti became louder and clearer, encouraging my return home spiritually. They began to speak through the many veterans I was honored to work with. My experience at Wayland stirred the underpinnings of recognition, not only of my culture but of my ancestral birthright. As I began the study/discovery process of my own ideology, fundamental psychology became more of the focus. This stemmed from the thousands of hours I spent with brothers and sisters returning from combat assignments and their families, helping restore their lives and create new coping mechanisms. However, the more I studied, the more Óðinn revealed to me my role in this world. He gave the vision to see through the coverings and identify the population control protocol that created the foundation for monotheism.

Throughout my life, while I was busy attempting to forge my own path, the Landvætti worked fervently to align certain events and interactions with individuals to assist in guiding my decision matrices back to where they needed to be to align with the path my inner self wanted to be on. Although my use of "free will" had created large gaps between where I found myself and the path my spiritual self knew I should travel, the data that my decisions were based on was fundamentally flawed.

However, Hel couldn't let me escape from her grasp and cursed my wife with breast cancer several years later. Together, my shield maiden and I put our shoulders into it and conquered cancer. That was over twelve years ago, and she continues to honor me daily with her beautiful soul.

However, when Hel realized that cancer wouldn't break us, she led me to the path of infidelity through temptation. Although I never physically strayed, I mentally violated my oath to my wife. Again, with the heart of Frigg, my wife forgave me, and we continued our process forward. While we have become closer as time moves on, I know the challenges of Hel's attempt to break me and my family remain in both the physical and spiritual worlds. I have continually sought Óðinn's grace since those darker days.

Fast forward to about 2018, when my mother asked me to assist with her genealogy project. As I began to explore the documentation and bloodlines, more fog was lifted from my eyes. I found my great-grandmother and great-grandfather. My great-grandmother was born in Jutland, Denmark, with my great-grandfather being born across the border in Germany. Many of the pieces I was missing in my life began to coalesce.

About the same time as I was working on our genealogy, I was called on by two individuals who had recently returned home from tours overseas. As we addressed ways for them to cope with their overwhelming symptoms, the powers of Óðinn became obvious, and I was afforded an opportunity to further explore the spiritual realm for knowledge. Those individuals received a lifetime of success via the gods because I was able to channel the words of Óðinn.

The exploration into other realms incited me to continue my research on spiritual interactivity with humans. I delved into the development of human cognitive thought, the natural evolution of man and environment, and the rise and fall of multiple theologies.

One of the largest challenges within any spiritual practice is to remember to keep it simplistic and comfortable. Spirituality should come to us naturally, without conflict or discipline. In many practices, individuals will seek methods to cause division and distrust among the practitioners in-lieu of unity and harmony. Some might say that even the content within this book speaks of division and distrust, but my intention is to help people understand this is simply another interpretation of what you already know. Not better, not worse, just different. The best method of obtaining an in-depth understanding of our interpretations is by drilling down past the detailed "practice" narratives as deeply as possible, particularly the ones that only the church leadership understands. This has been the mainstay for the enforcement of all monotheistic practices since their inception.

Help Along The Way

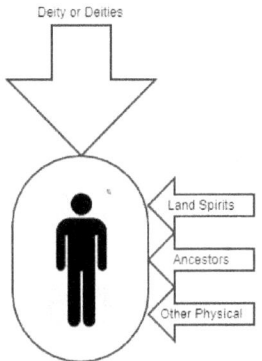

Figure 2 - *There are a plethora of entities we interact with on a spiritual level every minute of every day.*

The good news is that the spiritual world's inhabitants want to help us be successful. Throughout our physical existence, we retain a constant connection with spiritual resources who are willing and able to guide us through the many emotional challenges that we face. This assistance comes in different forms. We can call upon physical individuals who are more receptive to the other realms of existence, such as shamans, druids, or ministers, or we can seek out the spiritual entities in our search for answers. The idea of setting aside one's ego and insecurities to employ others for help is the first step in moving past the practice you were raised under and embracing a more spiritually centric existence.

Another piece of good news is that it really doesn't matter what the name says above the door as to whether you should be open to it or not. All indigenous beliefs are centered around several key factors. These will be discussed at length a little later, but ultimately the idea that we understand the spiritual connection that each of us possess, and how that connection affects our everyday lives is what is important. Remember, there is no wrong answer, only a better understanding.

There are a multitude of spiritual entities who have access to us on this plane of existence via a plethora of connection methods. Some of these entities have had a physical lifetime and therefore understand emotions. Because there are a great number of these entities, there is a substantial potential of at least one with an identical experience to ours, meaning we can draw on their knowledge and experiences.

In a very limited case, there are several (I personally believe that there are at least two, but those are my own beliefs) deity-level individuals who possess the universal energy necessary for specific cases, such as the "create something from nothing" energies. In addition, these entities can show favor by granting additional energy to the fruition of prayers and spells (more about that later). These entities have the wisdom and knowledge of all that will ever be known; therefore, they are a powerful resource that our spiritual selves have direct access to.

The greatest step we can take in the quest for understanding is to actively seek. This includes another topic that we will cover in depth a little further in the book: intent. By applying the level of desire, or want, to those prayers and/or cast spells, we multiply exponentially the energy at which they move toward fruition. With all the help that we have available to us, and with the understanding of the necessary journey we have engaged upon, it begins to clear away the fog as to why we have chosen the physical existence path for our emotional education.

When discussing the concept of "seeking" we would be remiss if not mentioning that because every life form on the physical plane has a spiritual source, they too can be a resource to draw upon for wisdom and knowledge. While we will discuss the personal aura in a later chapter, understanding that there are those around us who wish to interact at a deeper level, seeking and offering knowledge and wisdom that they might not be aware of themselves.

However, in the search for those who can or will assist us in understanding our lessons of this physical existence, we must be cognizant of those who have halted their spiritual growth by adopting the superficial idea of the practice as a theology. By believing the necessity of "converting others" and/or forcing others to believe in a narrative that does not provide them intrinsic comfort, those individuals are subscribing to a practice and not the theology itself. The influence of practice on the human race has had catastrophic impacts on society throughout all of recorded history.

In our quest to understand the spiritual influences that will affect our lives from time to time, we need to clearly delineate the difference between an actual theology and the practice that developed around those core beliefs. Forced practices have had a negative impact on spirituality.

Influence of Practice

Before taking a deep dive into understanding my lessons in separating the practice from the theology, I need to assure you, the reader, that I do not condemn any understanding of spirituality that has ever existed throughout the history of humans. However, I believe that we must understand the "elephant in the room" when it comes to modern day religions of the world and the unfortunate manipulation of truth to arrive at what many define as the negative narrative.

Having said that, I must admit that I, like many others, am frustrated by the implementation of the practices that seem to have become affiliated with the major organized religions. Our definition of an "organized" religious practice comes primarily from the Middle East. Although much of its initial growth was limited to Eastern Europe, it quickly spread because of its initial fluidity, and its perceived value to the ruling classes of the day. My definition of a "practice" is defined as action steps necessary to display one's faith in a recognized theology or belief system. It is the way we act when professing our faith to a particular religious affiliation. This idea becomes more central when considering the three mainstream monotheistic practices:

1. Judaism was the original monotheistic practice, originating about 3000 years before the current era. Originally bound to those of the Jewish clans, it fractured the underlying theology from the polytheistic beliefs dominant during the time. While it contains a substantial number of demonstrations of obedience, it is limited only to people of Jewish descent. Again, we find that the practice then began to quash rebellion and disobedience, forcing those of the appropriate ancestry to comply or pay a heavy price, limiting independent thought or worship.

2. Christianity was the first fracture of Judaism and also against the predominant polytheistic beliefs of the Roman Empire, allowing the "infidels" of the west to be "converted" to this modified version of Judaism. This was also the first evidence of a small group of people who determined the obedience displayed by those practitioners of Judaism could be enforced on the masses and began to enact control over people. The brutality of the enforcement within this practice would extend beyond the wildest imaginations of the original authors.

3. The Nation of Islam was, initially, a minimized distribution of "rules of behavior" and another fracture from Judaism that was limited (initially) to a smaller sect of the population starting around the seventh century of the current era. While they taught a religion of peace, the underlying mechanism of obedience was much more violent in nature.

I draw your attention to the use of the word "practice" within the above definitions, as they each brought a behavior modification "practice" with the proposed theology. The enforcement of these practices became the beginning of the end for the clearly defined theology, thereby creating a chasm between the underlying spirituality within a theology and the societal behavior permitted, possibly even encouraged. There begat a manipulation mechanism to control all behaviors, and while the theism behind these practices taught a message of peace and harmony, the practice and its enforcement began to take on a more violent, often deadly position.

The first manipulation of these "practices" was that there wasn't a tolerance defined or implemented for acceptance of other beliefs. This fact alone has caused more death and destruction than any other single facet of these practices. However, as more individuals interpreted the holy texts written by the earlier disciples, we found different interpretations as to what part of these holy texts were important. By translating the text differently, more methods to control behavior of the general population were identified. This process has continued for millennia.

In addition, some of the "practices" included within these newer teachings are a vicious circle of encouraging practitioners to "force" others within their social circle to adopt the same practice or be shunned. This included the condoning of mass murder of any belief practitioner who did not conform. As a very small sample, we can see where these "practices" were not conducive to co-existence or inclusion.

- The establishment of Christianity throughout Europe and Islam through the Middle East used force in almost every example to garner support from the populations of the area. Most often this was accomplished in a "top-down" exercise by securing the ruling classes of the day with several initiatives to encourage adoption of the practice, including:
    - Financial security. This practice secured goods and fiscal support from an economic class that would have been disagreeable to other requests for financial support. However, throughout all recorded history, we find the wealth of the world centered around these churches.
    - Population Control Mechanisms. By forcing the adoption of this new practice, mechanisms were placed on societies that elevated the ruling classes as "higher beings" appointed by a deity to rule. This reduced the potential for a revolt against the ruling classes. It fostered the guilt and shame cycle that continues today.
- The Crusades (1095 -1291) - The Christians of Europe attempted to dislodge the Muslim worshippers from the

perceived "birthplace" of the central figure in their narrative. This led to over 100 years of conflict and left hundreds of thousands dead in a failed attempt to usurp the locals. The reality was that it brought forward the concept of the martyr and made it common on both sides.

- The Puritans left England en masse from 1630 to 1642 to escape the persecution of their perceived "individuality" of worship practices. The underlying concept of individuals wanting to "practice" their faith differently would be another piece of evidence suggesting that people recognized the enforcement of certain practices to be of a critical necessity and realized the potential for them to put their own demands for obedience in place.

- The Salem Witch Trials (1692 - 1693) - We witnessed the level of practice enforcement of these settlers' beliefs that resulted in many deaths. This is another of the hundreds of events that demonstrate the ease of promoting the idea of "die or conform" type of enforcement that early settlers of the new nation adopted from the European mindset. According to historical records, this type of enforcement was often repeated.

- Trail of Tears (1830 - 1850) - The conquering Europeans drove the indigenous peoples west from their ancestral lands to pieces of land they thought were unusable. This act was primarily driven by the conformists who demanded that the natives surrender their beliefs, as well as a racist hue that colored their vision. Estimates declare that over 100,000 people lost their lives from this act of barbarism, all in a method of enacting control over others.

- In the 20th century, there are still groups abducting children into a "church run" education system, all in an attempt to "dissolve" the indigenous belief systems and ways of life, because they are different.

These are just a few of the millions of instances where the early monotheistic churches enforced their practices with zero tolerance for other local beliefs. The "conform or die" mentality has persisted since the inception of these monotheistic practices.

I want to be very clear that these examples are defined within the "practice" and not the underlying theology. While my examples are about the Christian church, the Nation of Islam, as well as Judaism, has had a very similar history with their adhere or suffer tactics as well. These have become the markers on the road to individuality destruction that clearly demonstrates the difference between the theology (or beliefs) and the practice (displayed actions). These systems rose to influence about the same time that a substantial amount of human migration was happening in the world sometime around the transition to the current geological epoch. A clear line of division emerged between behavior and beliefs, and the beliefs were minimized to implement behavior manipulation strategies by the architects of the modern monotheistic practices.

Hopefully, getting the negative stigma out of the way early will allow us to continue with an open mind and relieved heart that you are not the only one who has pondered the societal impact organized religions have had on the general population. While this may seem as a negative toward the monotheistic religions of the world, it is not intended to be. It is intended to help us draw the distinction between the underlying spiritual beliefs and the enforced practices. However, it is critical to understand spiritual beliefs can be covered through enforced practice by anyone who wishes to weaponize it. Organized religions frequently have exploited the population's confusion over the mysterious powers of the natural world and attempted to elevate their own status at the cost of the people.

Had the early shamans who accepted the responsibility of communicating with the spiritual world adopted a similar practice, the world might have been different. The early shamans who migrated with their tribes across the Beringia Land Bridge before it submerged with the rising sea waters, and those spiritual guides who migrated across the many different paths out of Africa, recognized the spiritual influences around them and used their communications to the betterment of their tribe. They recognized the value of providing knowledge to foster the adoption of beliefs and not promote the conformity enforcement that religion would become. They accepted the responsibility to help their tribes remain "in balance" with the world. Later in the book, we'll discuss ways we can seek this same balance.

Spirituality is based around an idea of understanding "the self" by revealing the connection between the spiritual and physical selves. While many struggle to recognize this connection, by deploying methods of self-focus, we can begin to reveal these inputs into our psychology, or those thoughts that make us, us. Hopefully your investigation into the principles of this book gives you insight to catapult your personal happiness through peace and harmony with the spiritual world around you, as well as the connection between your selves.

Thankfully, spiritual beliefs are alive and well in the modern day, and they are even enjoyed by many who practice monotheistic worship, and there is absolutely nothing incorrect or inaccurate about that. If one can delineate between the actual theology and the encouraged societal practices of a particular religion, then we find that we are all on the same playing field and are well on the way to seeking our destiny as a wonderful, unique understanding of truth.

Seeking Our Destiny

One of the strongest forces within the physical plane is the power of intent, and while it may sound simplistic, it can be the most challenging of all the obstacles we face on this plane of existence. The idea behind intent is a measurement of the desire behind a request. We can see this later during the chapter on Prayers, Worship & Magic; however, it drives all things. Many people choose to let life happen, accepting their fate in a victim mentality. But within this life, we are meant to have more of a commanding role. When we actively seek, we will find. For those among us who seek division and mistrust, they will find it everywhere, as there are always ways to divide and segregate. However, those who seek commonality, harmony, and peace can find it everywhere.

Our necessity to balance the spiritual existence with physical action steps, places the activity of "seeking" in the action side of the equation, meaning that for those who pray (or cast spells), then follow up with an action of "seeking" the answer, will more than likely discover the results they desire. I would also add that, although many here on earth have told me "Money may not buy happiness, but it makes the wait more tolerable," materialistic gains are not existential and therefore will remain here on the physical plane when we move back to the spiritual realm at the conclusion of this physical lifetime.

Fate is one of the functions that has been assigned to the Landvætti. By listening with one's heart, we can arrive at a transient state within our mind where we convince the self to force a change in our life's trajectory. In other words, fate is a call to action, a call from the spiritual self to the biological self to act. The Landvætti can provide the roadmap to our existence that meets the lowest level of emotional intellect necessary to move past this physical lifetime. It is up to each of us to engage this intent to align our lives to our destiny of emotional understanding.

Destiny is another one of those spiritually orientated buzzwords that we frequently hear when discussing one's life goals. Ultimately, all physical lives have a destiny of leaving the physical world to join our ancestors within the spiritual realm. But, in addition, our destiny is to create a spiritual memory of emotional experiences to help our descendants who experience similar situations and need guidance. By creating a controlled emotional knowledge and wisdom, we are then better suited to offer suggestions to those still living a physical existence. To say that someone is "destined" to be a King or have superpowers would be a physical plane manifestation, whereas the reality is we are all here to learn emotional control, and thereby, empathy toward others.

Cultural Influences

In today's world of uncertainty, many are seeking a path to understanding their spirituality. In some cases, we find individuals associating with their ancestry in a fervent attempt to fulfill the void left by their recent revelation of a lifetime spent in the worship of a practice instead of the necessary theology.

For the most part, our individual spirituality is based tightly around these cultural associations. This is not by accident. Throughout history, spiritual understandings have been created regionally by individual clans. These independent beliefs then aligned with other beliefs because of the direct interaction between the shamans and the spiritual entities of that time and space; however, they developed individually. If we research the indigenous beliefs around the world, particularly around the end of the last ice age (about 11,000 years ago), we can see where many of the beliefs have a substantial number of common threads woven through them, even though they were thousands of miles apart. It is this commonality that I personally have discovered is where the reality of spiritual understanding is.

My Heritage

The necessity of understanding the connection between myself and my ancestors has taken on a newer, more substantial role in my life. Wrestling with where the many different beliefs I have in my mind came from required a substantial amount of prayer and spiritual channeling, as my immediate ancestors (mother and father) had determined that the values passed through the genetic markers mattered very little. Both my mother and father were born here in the United States: New Jersey and Pennsylvania respectively. My mother, the product of a long generational collection born here in the United States, with most being born within 350 miles of the state of West Virginia. My father, on the other hand, only had a single generation before him born here, immediately moving my personal ancestry to the lands of

Germany, Denmark, and Ireland. This intrigued me greatly, so I began to dig deeper into my personal ancestry. One of my paternal great-grandmothers was the product of more than twenty generations from their ancestral home in Denmark, while the other great-grandmothers were the product of more than twenty generations in Ireland. While one of my great-grandfathers was born in the States, the other was the product of many generations from western Germany.

Why is this important? At the core of my spiritual understanding was the need to recognize the influences on my definition of spirituality. It became critical for me to understand how my brain made sense of what I felt as I interpreted what I was being taught daily by my spiritual ancestors. The further back I traveled in time, the closer I found myself to my ancestors, understanding what they spoke of and what sense they had made of the world of their time. This allowed me to frame a context within my mind to begin to understand the wisdom they imparted to me.

After my experience with meeting Óðinn that evening in my backyard, the necessity of putting into place what it meant became my obsession. I began, in earnest, to put the missing pieces together to understand why I thought the way I did. My intrinsic beliefs began to take shape within the framework of what would become the "legends of the north" and ultimately, the Vikings of Denmark.

My personal ancestry could potentially be traced back to the Sámi people along the northern shore of Finland and Sweden, where their indigenous shamanistic practices would be upheld for thousands of years, surviving to the modern day. My connection to my ancestors really begins when the Gaels ruled over what is today the Iberian Peninsula (France and Spain) until about 100AD when they were conquered by the Romans. Many years later, others changed the leadership again in the area. However, we see the Celtic culture migrate and evolve. Different from our ancestral heritage and biological ancestry, this culture incorporated the daily practices of the people with the understanding of the spiritual realm that co-existed with us. The Celts. Slow at first, the Celts conquered most of Europe as we know today and cast their influence on different practices and beliefs throughout the world. As the Celts migrated north and northwest from what is today France, they migrated through the area known then (originally coined by the Romans) as Germania. Many Celts migrated south to warmer climates, but a substantial number traveled north, eventually crossing the Elba River to join another Germanic tribe of the area: the Danes. This is where my story really begins to take shape. This crossover between the early Celtic beliefs and the Norse mythology resonated in my mind and explained the feelings in my heart.

While I believe in more than one god (polytheistic beliefs of the Norse), I recognize the power of the spiritual energy around us every day (animistic beliefs of both the Sámi peoples and many of the Celt tribes). While I may use the labels used by my Norse ancestors, I also recognize the infinity for which the gods are, therefore understand that other labels may be used by other peoples, and then realize that it only begins to scratch the surface of understanding infinity.

With all that said, let me demonstrate what I mean by my understandings being more open to inclusion:

1. I believe there are a minimum of two gods. One of these gods is the masculine, the other feminine. This distribution of energies creates balance within the universe. All things have a dark and light, life and death, all things within the universe are in balance.
2. I believe that the spiritual entities who join us on this realm of existence come in two forms; again, note the balance:
    a. The first group is the Landvætti, or land spirits. These spirits can be found in the winds, the sun, the moon, the seasons, as they have many functions. They contain the knowledge and wisdom of what will be known throughout eternity.
    b. The second group is our ancestors. All our ancestors. Every form of life that has ever had a spiritual self. All

living things have a spiritual self, so upon departing their physical existence, they traverse the spiritual realm.
3. I believe that everyone will depart their physical selves at the end of its life and move to the spiritual existence where they may choose to stay or return to the physical existence in another physical form.
4. I believe that everyone is responsible for their spiritual and emotional education, and although I may offer advice, they are free to use it or not. Their choice has no bearing on our relationship.

While the discovery of my ancestral roots filled in gaps within my understanding, the staunch realization I have come to embrace is the idea of not having a religion. My spiritual beliefs are associated with my culture; therefore, I am not a religious practitioner but a cultural subscriber, which is why it was so important for me to discover what that entailed. What had it meant to be Celtic? Or Norse?

One of the first big understandings I realized and struggled with was the understanding that another entity's acceptance of my culture no longer mattered. It is fine if others do not embrace my beliefs and practices. As a long-time servant of modern monotheistic practices, "saving" others was a defined part of my obedience. However, my spiritual entities taught me, had this been the case throughout time, older understandings from pre-Christian Europe would have survived, but alas, as they have been completely removed from the minds of our ancestors, that did not happen. Like us, they cannot be forced to change their hearts to believe something incongruent with who they are. I believe this is the most difficult portion I had with letting go of my previous practices and beliefs.

This freedom of thought brought me to the place where I understood the societal brainwashing that had taken place over the millennia. I recognized it for what it was. By creating a need for each practitioner to constantly seek to "convert" their social influences, not only did they potentially increase the obedience of a larger group, but failures to convert allowed for additional intrinsic guilt to be accumulated, thereby increasing the dependency of each practitioner. Understanding the impact that this had on society over the millennia opened my eyes to their misunderstanding of an infinite being.

During my vision with Óðinn that night in my backyard, we spoke of my father, and his father, turning away from their ancestral birthright and denying their culture to secure the material riches of the modern day. Neither chose to follow any religion and attempted to remove the rich culture from the following generations. My grandfather prevented it from being passed to my father, who then did his best to conceal it from me. It wasn't until I found it later in my life that I restored our culture to our family line. Thankfully, there are people like you and I who are willing to restore these rich cultures to the center of people's lives as they were intended to be.

Arrival At An Understanding

This brings us to the understanding that a valuable part of a culture is its spiritual understandings and beliefs. This understanding drives the practice, which is exhibited through public displays as well as private thoughts and beliefs. This is what culture is. Culture is spiritual beliefs displayed as behaviors as well as the desires of the people to hold on to their ancestral heritage.

Why Are We Here?

This is an age-old question, and although we've received the answer a million times, we continue to seek additional comfort in the answer that our heart knows is right. As spiritual entities, we spend a physical lifetime on this plane of existence to secure emotional intelligence with the goal of achieving emotional empathy toward others. We require a physical existence because the genetic chemistry that affects every piece of sensory data we receive alters the message created, thereby allowing us a distinct perspective than another entity who may have a different collection of genetic chemistry affecting their sensory input.

> "We are spiritual entities that inhabit a biological body on a temporary plane of existence in an effort to learn the necessary emotional control to obtain an empathetic mind to further the peaceful existence of others."
>
> -Alaska *Úlfhéðnar*

The emotional manipulation of the data received by the mind creates an unfortunate disadvantage. Many fully developed belief systems are constructed based on the relatability of the brain, which can incorrectly acquire potentially corrupted data pieces. This essentially builds a house of cards. When one underlying piece of data is proven inaccurate, there is the potential of a cascading effect, drawing suspicion to all the related data points within our memory, which may cause irreparable damage to the thought capabilities. This cascading effect can cause a psychological impact that then severely hampers any further processing of data, causing further data loss and corruption. This is one of the major reasons why we are here on earth, to better understand the emotional impact of data points that become our knowledge, and ultimately our wisdom, that we can offer to others on the physical plane as empathy.

While many toss around this question as a punchline at the social club, it underscores the idea that humans have become so arrogant and egocentric to the point of total loss of true spiritual understanding. This same arrogance led to the implementation of socially detrimental practices throughout millennia that attempted to reshape our life goals into something more usable by these controlling forces. While many have chosen to relax and wait for success to find them, we need to actively seek our destiny.

The key to our spirituality is that we are in charge of the journey we take through our physical lifetime. We can allow our chemical imbalances to determine our path, or we can take control by building mechanisms into our daily routine that allow us to take back control and eradicate emotionally charged memories stored by the brain. These emotional landmines are a major cause of instability and unreliability of our auric projection into the spiritual realm and therefore alter our base knowledge as well as our potential for creating the reality we desire.

While many can get stuck in a vicious cycle here, being in control of our lives by exercising our free will can alter our trajectory at any point. Instead of accepting the victim role, we have a choice. A choice to take this emotional lesson, learn it, then toss aside the associated guilty memories to alter our trajectory and become successful. Remember, ultimately our goal on earth is to learn as much as we can about the control of chemical interactions called emotions and become an empathetic master.

How has it come to this? The answer takes a couple of hundred thousand years to fully understand, as we must seek to better understand what each of the evolutionary steps we, as human beings, have taken to reach where we are now.

EXERCISES

Chapter 1: Absorbing the Energy of this Wisdom

Throughout this section, we've identified how I acquired this knowledge and what intrinsic knowledge I am using to fully explore and explain a true understanding of spirituality. There are many parts to accepting and understanding our spirituality; however, identifying the many fragments of knowledge is where we need to start. To better help you incorporate this wisdom or better your understanding into your current beliefs, here are some exercises. Make note of the following questions and jot down your answers after deliberate concentration on each. We'll review some answers in the next section to help illuminate your path to enlightenment.

1. What is your personal defined difference between spirituality and religion, or are they the same?
2. Does being a non-believer of religion disconnect you from spirituality?
3. What does spirituality mean to you? Is it a doctrine (Christian, Muslim, Buddhists, etc.) associated with a church somewhere? Is it a natural part of life with or without humankind?
4. If you say you are having a "spiritual experience", what does that mean to you?
5. Do you explore spirituality by yourself? Does anyone else have to be present for you to experience your definition of spirituality?
6. What is your definition of a "god"?
7. How do we recognize the influence of our ancestors?

This list of questions is a start in your journey of dissecting your beliefs and challenging what you think you believe. I provided a sample to build from, but each question should generate others. The questions I don't want you to have are, "why is he asking this" or "how do I answer correctly?" When we are more interested in the rights and wrongs, we lose sight of the true wisdom in the universe available when we drop the labels from our thought process.

Remember, when working with spirituality, there are no right or wrong answers, there is just "our truth" or our perception of the truth. We believe different things because of the experiences we've had throughout our existence. Even before our physical forms took shape, we have had the experiences of being in the spiritual realm. Ultimately, we are seeking to understand why we believe the things we do and whether those beliefs still serve us today.

Are our beliefs a reflection of where we *were*, or are they where we *want to be*?

Each of the questions should have garnered some answer or series of answers. Let's explore each answer further.
1. Why do I believe this?
2. Who taught me this? Are they trustworthy with my faith?
3. Is there an emotional connection to this knowledge?
4. Have I changed my spiritual beliefs? Why?

By dissecting your answers, you are beginning an in-depth search for several things. First, you are asking yourself if the "current you" thinks the data point makes total sense. In all that you know, are your beliefs logical? Could you defend it against anyone else's contrary belief? Obviously, being willing to stand alone is the most powerful signature that your belief is genuine and meets your criteria for your belief system. By accepting the path we have traveled as a journey of knowledge gathering and experiences, we must accept them for what they are: a learning exercise constantly teaching us where destiny wants us to travel.

Second, after making sense to us, does the belief feel acceptable to the heart? How do you feel about this belief? The emotional responses to the questions, and more particularly, the answers, are another part of the answer. When we have emotional associations with our memories, we need to ask why. By disconnecting our negative emotional association to a particular sensory input, we fully understand the physical existence. If you are ambivalent about the hard belief, consider further evaluation. Again, we are looking for beliefs that we can obtain congruence with, and this congruence occurs when the heart and mind align with their acceptance of the belief.

➔ Ask question -> derive answer -> determine emotional response -> Ask why emotional response -> continue.

Through this piece-by-piece method, we can begin to understand what we believe and why we believe it. A major piece of these exercises is attempting to brush aside our ego, and our bravado, to be honest with ourselves. Once we establish our understanding of our personal belief system, our auxiliary thought processes will begin to make sense.

Adopting The Successful Wisdom Using Meditation

To thoroughly comprehend the wisdom and knowledge passed to us from elders and ancestors, we must embed the new information deep within our psyche to determine when the data received meets the necessary burden of proof for our heart and our mind in concert.

If you haven't done meditation before, I'd like to offer some ideas.

Don't believe anything you've heard or seen on television or the internet. The idea of meditation does not necessarily mean we assume some painful looking pose, burn incense, smoke dope, visit some remote location, or any other nonsense. We simply want to limit our physical sensory input (sight, sound, smell, taste, or feel) and relax. There is no wrong way to meditate. Without the physical senses, we can allow our mind to wander within itself and see what happens. Typically, when one first begins to meditate, it can be challenging to minimize external events from entering the mind. This is where the concentration part comes in. By having an easy to remember topic, we can coerce the mind back to focusing on what we want to know and not reliving today's events.

Our meditation topic for this section is the discovery of the formation of our beliefs. Focus on each question above, spend time focusing on that question, and see what thoughts come to you.

What do you feel?

Sometimes our emotional connection may be significant, thereby invoking an emotional response. Sometimes the visions or thoughts may seem completely arbitrary or muddled. These are all responses to note. This is completely normal. Again, you'll want to spend about 30 minutes pondering each question. Note what you feel and think as the question is brought up in your mind.

The final part will be to compare your answer notes after meditation with the answers you provided initially in the questions section above. Again, exercise patience, as it may take a few meditation sessions to garner enough mind control to minimize the influence of external intrusions into our thought process and get some response. The key here is not to get discouraged. It may take a little time to begin to clear away this fog.

Chapter Two

The Evolution of the Self

To understand where we, as human beings, have come from and why we are here, we need to understand the intelligent design which I believe is how we have come to be. There is too much scientific evidence that points to our constant ability to adapt and evolve to discount it as the methodology that has gotten the human race to where it is today.

Many have accepted the ideology within different practices that teach of deities creating "completed" humans, one man and one woman. I believe this is a misunderstanding. The "completed" interpretation intends to imply these "original humans" were not designed to evolve and change; however, we find too much contradictory evidence in the historical record, whether we are identifying the arrival of the initiation of evolution from before the time of those first two anatomical modern humans. The evolution theory coincides with the historical record as anthropology demonstrates how humans have evolved over the millennia. If we also take into consideration the other life forms that share the physical plane with us, we can clearly see a defined evolution and adaptation that has occurred and continues to occur today.

Figure 3 - *As humans evolved, so too did their capacity of thought.*

I personally think that our infinite beings (deities) would have implanted two biological bodies that possessed the power of evolution, and therefore these first humans possessed the genetic capabilities of further evolving over time. When speaking about the evolution of humankind, we need to be cognizant of two essential pieces of this evolution. The first is of the biological unit we inhabit on the physical plane, and the other is our spiritual self, which forms before the conception of our biological self. These individual parties are then bound together for a physical lifetime of emotional experiences that continue to alter them and their offspring for generations. We need to embrace this physical understanding to fully comprehend the uniqueness of who we are and what we will become.

Physical Entity Evolution

Some may wonder why a book about spirituality contains a section about the evolution of humans. The reality is that we need to understand the influence our biological body has on our spirituality, or more importantly, what influence our spirituality has on our human psychologies. Herein lies the challenge of the human-to-spirit connection that occurs, understanding the influences and/or adaptations that one will have on the other. While we have an idea that there must be a physical organ called the soul, and while the idea might be good, the reality is that our soul is technically our spiritual self. A separate yet joined part of our personality, our intelligence, our wisdom, every part of our physical body is associated with the "self" that is our spiritual part. We need to consider how the human evolutionary path has led us to understanding what we know today.

All intrinsic spirituality that we know of today is what remains after a split of the instinctual thought processing held long before the Anatomical Modern Humans (AMH) evolved from their ancestors in what is today northeast Africa. While the other physical plane lifeforms retained their instinctual, strong spiritual connection, the evolution of cognitive thought within the human form redirected their thought process, creating an inherent challenge of accessing the underlying spiritual connection, thereby separating their connection to other lifeforms around them. This revealing of the spiritual connection, from a processing perspective, attempted to recover some of the functions formerly completed by the instinctual thought process by extending our aura further out and making it more sensitive. In addition, our ancestors attempted to rely on spiritual entities for insight and wisdom, and while some witnessed great success, many others came to depend on other, more receptive individuals throughout their group, such as shamans and medicine practitioners to interpret these mysterious powers of the natural world.

As evolution continued and experiences were gained, we find the expansion of our (humankind) cognitive thinking commanding more of the brain processing abilities, ultimately eliminating our instinctual thought process almost completely. Today, the use of instinct is almost entirely reserved for life preservation.

The evolution of our psychology stems from cognitive thought process that happened within humans as more synapses were created within the human brain, approximately the same time the historical record shows the migration out of Africa hundreds of thousands of years ago[1]. With the further development of their ancestral methods of harnessing fire, the resulting advanced food preparation led to the easier digestions of proteins, of which we find the development of

---

1   There is some debate as to whether the Anatomical Modern Humans who migrated out of Africa had cognitive thought before migrating or discovered after.

FOXP2. Some may argue about its importance, however, there are many critical effects of this protein within the human body.

The Forkhead Box Protein (expressed genetically as FOXP2) began to multiply exponentially the number of synapses in the human brain, which led to greater cognitive thought, and my theory is that these increased synapses fostered the "relational" associations with the brain. Now, I'm not willing to debate the importance of brain cells contrasted against brain synapses; however, my theory is that the increase in synapses allowed us (humans) to associate one thing with another. This expanded relational data created the foundation for that process we call "wisdom". This cognition is still being debated in the anthropological/psychological scientific communities; however, I believe this is where we begin to see cause-and-effect type of thinking being utilized, and the ability to study and learn by deploying new methods of doing tasks continues the cycle of growing the capacity of this newly developed brain. This recognition of cognitive abilities would have begun the process of slowly reducing the instinctual thought process of our more animal ancestors by increasing the ability to apply this new type of cognitive and relational thinking.

The second part of the FOXP2 genetic expression would have provided the ability to genetically pass on these new brain synapses, meaning that the successive generations born continued to expand the thought capability in lieu of starting over. My own opinion is that the arrival of this protein and its integration into the genetic structure of human anatomy began a long evolution of ridding our psyche of the instinctual thinking that our ancestors had required for successful survival, as well as separate humans from the remainder of the physical plane inhabitants.

As evolution continued through thousands of generations, intermixed with varied and newer diets, the genetic manipulation continued to peel away the layers of instinctual thinking, exposing the deeply rooted spiritual connectivity that lied beneath. The more of this spiritual cognition that was revealed, the more dependent our ancestors became on the spiritual entities who assisted them in understanding the natural world.

> "… and so ignorant are we in spite of all our shamans that we fear everything unfamiliar…"
> "Therefore, we have customs, which are not the same as those of the white man. The white men who live in another land and have needs of other ways."
>
> -Knud Rasmussen 1930 Vol 7, No. 2:54-56

As societies became less dependent on the hunter/gatherer mentality, it continued to minimize the need for instinctual thinking, thereby revealing the need for an additional enhancement of sensory input from spiritual entities.

The anthropological record shows several evolutionary steps that have occurred between the primates and humans. What is so obvious to most is the amount of time elapsed that have occurred between these evolutionary steps. We must consider that most people are only familiar with the last couple of millennia. So, let's talk about the last million years. For ease of understanding, I've included the abbreviation below for "thousand years ago" with (kya).

Evolutionary Step	Estimated time of Existence
Homo heidelbergensis	700 kya – 200 kya
Early homo sapiens	300 kya – 45 kya
Homo Denisova	400 kya – 45 kya
Homo Neanderthalensis	400 kya – 40 kya
Anatomically modern humans (AMH)	200 kya – Present

According to the anthropological record, the generally accepted answer is that our ancestors discovered the harnessing of fire at about 300 kya, and the earliest Anatomical Modern Human discovery dates them to about 200 kya. This discovery would have led to the preparation of food, thereby enhancing the digestion process and making the Forkhead Box protein easily transferrable to the human genome. In addition, according to that same historical record, we know that when the modern humans migrated out of Africa, they integrated with the Neanderthals of Europe and Denisovans from Asia, and to a limited degree those early Homo Sapiens of what is today the Middle East. This combination continued to foster the evolution of the modern humans and increased the cognitive abilities throughout the many interactions.

The evolution of the biological body has been occurring for hundreds of thousands of years, which, to me, indicates the legitimacy of the evolution theory, noting specific historical findings that demonstrate the physical results in a multitude of findings all around the world. The explosion of the cranial capacity of humans that continued to enlarge from those earliest migrants to just short of the current day. However, for the sake of this discussion, I suggest that these humans were given the gift of intelligent design by the deities. This intelligent design allowed for this evolution and adaption to occur throughout the thousands of years.

At approximately 11 kya, the ice sheets receded and the water levels rose, ultimately leading to the submerging of the Beringia Land Bridge that extended between what is today northeastern Russia and northwestern Canada and Alaska. Soon after, we see in the historical record where humankind seemed to shift to a different mindset, focused more on agriculture/herding and a domesticated animal for food sources. This paradigm shift in the base psychology of our ancestors would have accelerated the removal of the instinctual thought process that our ancestors would have held until that point in history.

Another key understanding which will be controversial, but ultimately agreed upon by the scientific community, is that the evolution of humans included the fundamental alteration of our genetic construction. As diets were modified and the chemical manipulation of the system occurred, the base human genomes were modified. This modification continued as it was passed through the thousands of generations following. It is for this reason we find individuals at different levels of chemical influence than others. However, this alteration of our genetic code is a small part of what makes us who and what we are.

Genetic Modification

From our conception, our genetics are being altered by both intrinsic and extrinsic factors. Upon birth, our "blueprints" are stored within our deoxyribonucleic acid (DNA) passed to every cell within the human body, and it is being altered by many different conditions, including the hormones created by our body. This genetic mutation means that while we retain most of our ancestral genes, we modify many throughout our lifetime. This continues the evolution of the human biological body. We'll discuss some more about the importance of this manipulation later, however, we need to understand that, not only can we change our minds, but we can also re-write the genetic instructions as to what makes us, us. From the study identified below we can extrapolate that there are biological alterations happening to the human genome from the time an entity is conceived until the biological body fails. This alteration means that we have the biology within our own body to fundamentally change ourselves, as well as setting up our future generations to start at a better place than we did.

The method that allows our genes to reproduce is called mitosis (cell division), which is a normal biological process that is constantly occurring within our physical selves. Almost every type of cell within our body continues this process of splitting, then the original cell dies off, allowing the split cell to carry on the process. The splitting of our cells carries the code from the cell it split from. If that original cell is somehow modified or corrupt, then the newly split cell will be modified as well. We can see this in many ways; however, the most common representation of this process is the spreading of cancer cells throughout the body. While some cells may create a multitude of splits, and others may only create a few, the basic premise is that our physical bodies are in a constant state of repair and replacement. In the same way, if our hormone chemistry combination alters a cell structure, that too is then split and reproduced, multiplying the alteration in addition to passing it to an offspring.

Individual Creation

While much can be said about the creation of an entity, we need to understand that there are two parts to an individual on the physical plane.

1. Physiological or biological body that will transport us for a physical lifetime.
2. Spiritual eternal being who inhabits the physical body from just after conception until the biological death.

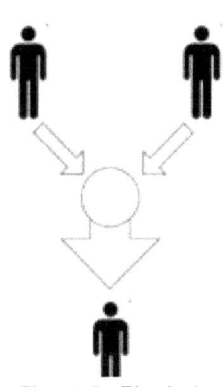

Figure 4 - *Physical conception is a straightforward process.*

The two sides are equally important, as the individual cannot live without either of these while the physical self is alive. While the physical side performs tasks and exercises the muscles of the physical form as well as providing the chemical composition necessary for recognizable emotions, the spiritual interactivity is equally important, as it provides an aura that interacts with the spiritual environment all around us.

To this point, the physical (or biological) body is created the same way we have been taught since we took "human development" in elementary school or were taught by our big brothers (Figure 4). This process described here is a little less detailed that those textbooks show us; however, it should include that there is a small portion of parental universal energy that is embedded during those moments where we witness the conception of an embryo. I'm not going to concern this book with the intricacies of human procreation, other than to say that these two small portions of universal energy passed to the embryo, one from each parent, establish a base level of connectivity to the spiritual realm. In addition, we find the mother providing the "intent" which supports the growth of the biological entity, as well as creating the vacuum to the spiritual realm, drawing a spiritual entity to this new biological conception. This draw from the spiritual realm creates a pull of a spiritual entity that, upon acceptance, lasts for a physical lifetime.

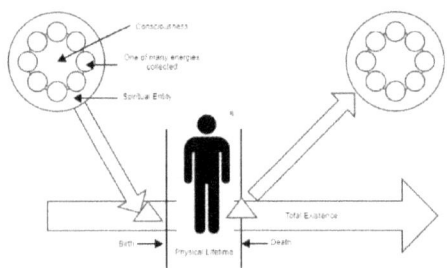

Figure 5 - *Our existence spends only a fraction in the physical plane.*

There are many different facets passed from parent to child, but none are more important than the genetic chemical adaptations made by the parental entity. We know, based on scientific evidence, that all physical entities make genome modifications throughout their lifetimes. These alterations are then passed to future generations, who alter it again during their lifetimes before passing it on to their offspring.

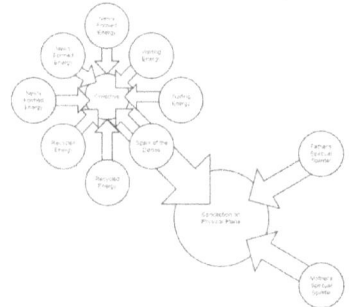

Figure 6 - *Spiritual entities are collections of universal energies that accumulate a consciousness.*

Spiritual entities are a little different throughout their creation process. Spiritual entities are created in the same manner that we will learn that is universal to all entities within all existences. Initially, they are unique and separate particles of energy suspended in the ether. They are drawn together using the magnetism of polarity until there is enough mass to obtain a consciousness and become self-aware. This is where the existence of an individual starts. At the same time, when the physical parental energy particles join during conception, a vacuum is created to the spiritual realm to draw a spiritual entity into bonding with the physical conception. This bonding exercise happens soon after conception of the biological body. Once the bonding is completed, then the spiritual entity and the biological entity are connected until the biological body fails. The two halves will spend the extent of the physical life span learning how to interact with each other as well as their surrounding environment.

Upon the biological demise, the first failure following expiration is the inability to manipulate the chemicals necessary to receive any further education. This inability to register any changes within the emotional state and create any energy within the physical mind is what fractures the bond between the spiritual and physical selves.

To further understand how this demise is registered by our spiritual self, we must understand the evolution of our psychology. While we have discussed the biological changes to our brain, and the slow revealing of our spiritual connection, we need to understand how we have come to process our thoughts. Our entire psychology is based on our sensory inputs; therefore, we need to grasp how this data is stored within our mind.

Physio-Psychological Evolution

To look at the psychological evolution, particularly with the human physical beings, we need to start back before the human thought process really happened. Before the Anatomical Modern Human (AMH), we find that the population would have had a more animal-like thought process, relying more on instinct and direct spiritual connection, with little or no cognitive thought capacity, essentially facing each situation as a new, separate event. The animal kingdom is much more in-tune with their spiritual surroundings than humans realize, as they are almost entirely interactive through their personal auras. While their thought process struggles to identify similar events, their spiritual interface allows for the explanation of the necessity of repeated activities. Instead of their brains focusing on storing the results of cause and effect, they rely completely on their spiritual interaction to provide the necessary instinctual response as it's needed. This is how the animal kingdom is different in thought process than evolved humans. This same process applies to other life forms here on the planet as well — plants, for instance, function the same way.

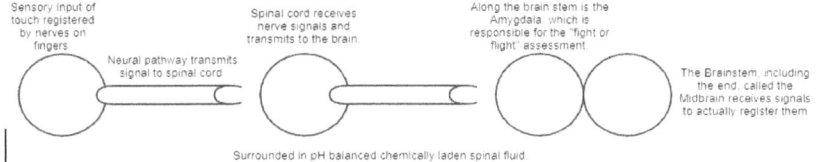

Figure 7 - *The neural path is entirely dependent on an acceptable chemical balance.*

During the psychological evolution of humans, we find the development of the sensory input process. Accepting sensory input from the multiple physical senses of the physical body, that input is managed, and/or altered with the use of the pH (potential hydrogen) balanced chemicals within the fluids surrounding the nerve endings, as well as the spinal cord with its fluid which extends into the brain. Every sensory input is managed in the same manner, thereby meaning our visual, auditory, olfactory, taste, and touch signals to the brain are all dependent on this chemical balance being within tolerable levels. For those who have altered their chemistry with intoxicating substances, this effect can be demonstrated, as our brain misinterprets many of the sensory input as the data will be transmitted through a different chemical makeup than the brain can process.

This chemically managed fluid alters signals received through it. In much the same way the mind can experience blind rage, or with grief, these chemicals alter the sensory input received by the brain, thereby altering the stored memory of that sensory input. In many cases, this explains the scenario of a multitude of people visually witnessing the same event yet having conflicting recollections of it. This chemical composition can prevent data from arriving at the brain at all, thereby "blacking out" the event completely. Most often, this happens when a witnessed event is overly traumatic to the intrinsic belief system, causing the brain to discard the input or simply disconnect any related connectivity, essentially storing it but removing accessibility to the memory.

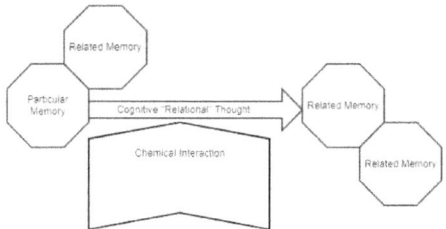

Figure 8 - *Individual memories have related memories within the brain.*

By transporting our sensory input on this chemically balanced fluid, we also allow for the input of spiritual sensory data to be added along the way. In the same way that physical sensory data is received by the brain, so too is the spiritual sensory data. Most often, the spiritual sense is mistranslated by the physical neural path and passed to the brain as physical sensory input, even though it isn't. This explains why many have reported seeing things, hearing things, or feeling things that cannot be validated by others but actually were on a different plane. Because the spiritual communications the physical self receives transmit across the neural pathways identically to our physical sensory input that most misinterpret the data received.

As the instinctual thought process is peeled back, revealing the spiritual connectivity, we find that the necessity of joining our collective self together becomes paramount. When attempting to communicate desires (either material, or knowledge based), we need to bind the two parts of the self together as the physical entities are unable to communicate with the deity realm or encourage other spiritual entities to assist in the fruition of either a prayer and/or cast spell, and therefore rely on the spiritual self to provide this function.

During the process of creating a vacuum for either knowledge and/or a desire, the interactivity between the physical self with the spiritual self is a critical first step. By connecting to our spiritual self, we can communicate with other spiritual entities more easily, as well as experience necessary interactions with either the deities or Landvætti for the completion of the vacuum.

To understand the growth of cognition, we can look at two modern day scenarios. I don't see these scenarios in the same manner; however, their exponential grasps for knowledge and understanding are similar in nature, as is their connection to their spiritual core. In addition, because of the decreased timeline to accomplishment, we can visualize the exponential growth of the cognition and stripping of instincts.

Figure 9 - *Understanding the connection between the selves, and our deity is very important.*

Infant/Toddler/Young Child. As a physical entity is born into the world, they must immediately set about the task of understanding the surrounding world. They must first master the use of the physical body, with some things such as eating and breathing being instinctual, while fervently trying to understand language (physical sensory input). Then they will arrive at the "cause and effect" thinking, and much later they will arrive at cognitive thought. A lot must be absorbed in short order for the human/spirit bond to be cemented into its trajectory in its physical lifetime and obtaining successful initiation of our life's ambition begins. As we witness our children conquer landmarks in cognitive thought, we witness the process as their cognition comes to the forefront of their thinking, thereby reducing their dependency on instinctual thinking. While we can encourage their growth, there are boundaries as to how far we can push before they get their thought process moving by themselves. We all go through this process.

Household pet. While far less cognitive than that of a human child, the aging difference within a pet provides some situation processing clues as to how our evolutionary ancestors would have processed different events. This cognition recognition is visible, so we know that the evolution of our ancestors, following the discovery of cognitive thought, must have become a cycle of learn and re-learn for thousands of years. More importantly, we know the steadfast spiritual communication channel within the processing of the animal hasn't changed throughout the hundreds of thousands of years, because it has worked. Even though the dependency on their human counterparts has increased, their spiritual connection remains exactly the same.

While a previous existence on the physical plane by a spiritual entity may expedite this learning curve for the spirit of the physical body to some extent, there are manipulations that happen within this new chemical composition which may negate some of the benefit of that experience. With the instinctual process limited to a small subset of self-preservation in modern times, sensory data input becomes paramount in newly formed lives.

Theological Evolution

What would a book about spirituality be without the understanding of how a theology emerged from the days before humans gained cognition? This is really a tough concept, and it is not until one understands the animal kingdom's interpretation of "then and now" that we begin to discover the core beginning of what would become theology. My discovery of a communication channel between a spiritual animal and myself led to an understanding of how the first hominids would have considered all things spiritually.

The animal kingdom has a simplistic thought process, and it is primarily based in what we'll call "instinctual thought". Instinctual thought is typically a straight path between the sensory input and the brain, meaning that, if an animal should smell you, they react. This process is referred to as instincts by modern science, but for the animal kingdom, it is simply what is. This instinctual thought process is where the first humans found themselves reacting to events and experiences within their environment, using their physical sensory input to see, hear, smell, taste, and touch physical things around them. However, buried deep within the instinctual thought process is a spiritual connection channel of receiving. This spiritual connection dominates the animal kingdom's thought processes, as it assists with the extension of their individual aura in directions it needs to go.

This spiritual channel allows the animal kingdom to communicate to other entities here on the physical plane, as well as the spiritual plane, using their individual auras. You may recognize this as the reason some animals respond differently to individuals. Depending on the interaction between that entity's aura and the animal's aura, a concern within the animal's mind may surface. Using the same interpretation of a spiritual input as they do for the physical body's sensory input, this simply becomes a reply to the perceived threat. This spiritual channel that the animal kingdom recognizes interacts with every other animal, plant, and human on the physical plane using this deep-seated spiritual connection. The animal kingdom simply accepts this communication as "what is".

As humans evolved from their instinctual thinking and use more cognition, different things began to have different meanings. For all intents and purposes, the world they lived in had many experiences that were beyond immediate understanding. This led to the consideration that there might be something larger out there that could either be against them or with them, depending on the situation. The natural world and its phenomenon can be quite intimidating and therefore needed explanations.

When a member of the clan was able to create fire by smacking two rocks together, an association was made that could explain the "large streaks of fire across the sky when the water fell down", thereby with the simplicity of experience association, someone, or something much bigger was doing the same thing. This thought process would expand to include the explanation of winds as something blowing air into their faces, and so on. Each small nugget of explanation that didn't have an immediate "cause" to see the effect became associated with this larger (unseen) person or thing.

Initially, we can say that the very first cognitive thought about this unseen figure would have defined it as monotheism. We find in most of the earliest indigenous beliefs there is a singular "creator" figure central to their understanding. So, this is where we see the development of "theology" as we understand it. Obviously, since this unseen agent was large enough to send fire streaks through the sky, our ancestors would have wanted to be sure that this entity would not destroy them, therefore we can see where the thoughts of respect and reverence stemmed from.

Prior to and during the blossoming of the cognitive thought capability, we know most of these humans still relied on their buried spiritual channel for communications with the many spirits who surrounded them. They recognized their ancestors' voices and presences and listened with their auras for the aura of others, validated by enhanced physical sensory input, determining the necessity for fight or flight.

As the associations continued to mount, the monotheistic belief system gradually recognized the deity level entity in addition to the spiritual world that continued to communicate through this buried channel. As cognition evolved, the collection of spiritual connections became recognized as a "deity level" entity and formed polytheistic beliefs.

From these early beliefs, we find the energy of the indigenous beliefs around the world possessing a recognized connection to the spiritual entities within other nearby life forms. We find the idea of the sacred feminine and guidance of the masculine resonate throughout most of these. From the early feminine goddesses to the understanding of "Mother Earth", these beliefs embraced the necessity for balance. As we survey these early indigenous peoples and their practices, common threads begin to emerge. These common threads will be what I refer to as the Universal Truths.

In summary, all theology started as a form of monotheism directly associated with animistic (meaning that they recognized the spirits around them and in everything), and the animal kingdom still recognizes that today. Cognitive thought brought into focus the associations of visible tasks that replicated natural phenomenon, thereby drawing attention to a single entity capable of replicating the small tasks on a global scale. From that we find a form of monotheism and more of the indigenous type of beliefs. In most of the indigenous understandings, there is an evolution of spiritual entities with a central "creator" who creates all things and surrounding spirits who inhabit all living things. Finally, we find a compilation of monotheism with animism, culminating in what is polytheism, which is the belief that each spirit is a deity level entity, and thusly associating gods to individual tasks.

Recognition of Theological Thought

Drawing on a vision provided to me from the Landvætti, I am shown how the early peoples arrived at the simplistic concept of something larger than themselves. First, we should always recognize that the spiritual center that is part of the animal kingdom would have existed in our ancestor's ancestors as well. However, the discovery of the harnessing of fire would also lead to an understanding of their theology.

Imagine being in a cave back before time really mattered. In the days where early humans were evolving and migrating out of northern Africa across the lands to the east, north, west, and south. Arriving in our cave shelter with today's harvest of gathered food sources, both plants and animals. Someone within our group begins the process of creating the fire for cooking and for warmth. They gather two handheld rocks together and strike them together. This strike causes a spark to travel through the open space to the tinder gathered around the logs that would burn. This spark would become significant when those same people were out in nature during the rains. A lightning strike followed by claps of thunder would seem very similar to the starting of the fire back in the cave. As cognition developed, a theory arose that a much larger entity was doing the same thing: creating the spark (or lightning strike), followed by the thunder (sound of the rocks being struck together). This would potentially have formed the first cognitive ideas of a larger being.

This same mindset would go on to explain the winds and other phenomenon in the natural world.

Who Are We?

This is an age-old question that has plagued humankind since we started walking in an upright position. Why do I think the way I do? Are these thought patterns given to me genetically, or are they a chemical composition within my body manipulating what I think I know?

They are both.

As talked about in an earlier section, the expression of FOXP2 in the human genome allowed for the passing of brain capacity on to the offspring. In addition, I mentioned the "parental energy" being passed from physical parental bodies to the offspring. These two factors connect who I am in relationship to my biological ancestors through my DNA.

> *There are two important sides to my arrival at my cultural heritage. The first is the genealogical uncovering of a proud ancestral connection with Northern Germany, and Northern Denmark, and Southern Ireland. As I mentioned earlier, my mother had asked me to do some ancestral research to determine my father's side, as she was working on her own heritage. As I began to peel back the paternal*

generations of my ancestry, I already knew that we were of German descent; however, what wasn't clear at the onset was that my great-grandfather was born in Western Germany and came from a fairly long line of German born family members. As I searched through the church logs, I discovered generation after generation born within 150 miles of each other in Northern Central Germany.

At the same time, I discovered that one of my great-grandmothers was born in Jutland, Denmark, and the other in Northern Ireland. This led to the discovery of fifteen generations of ancestors born in Western Denmark, mostly in the Northwestern area around Bjereby Sogn. At the same time, fifteen generations were born in County Waterford, Ireland. This type of research can be difficult due to the availability of church records from that time period but discovering Danish and Irish ancestry dating back to the 1400s was thrilling. It stirred something deep inside my heart and mind, providing an intrinsic discussion as to my understanding of my ancestor's influence on my current day life.

While we may recognize that the genetic structure of our biological bodies is formed by the genome passed to the offspring from the biological parents, we can now understand that a fraction of every preceding generation's universal energy is also passed. These miniscule particles of universal energy can then make connections within the brain, thereby encouraging a particular thought process to emerge as dominant. In addition to altering our biological processing, I believe that this universal energy establishes a connection across the spiritual realm to our ancestry in addition to predisposing us to enhanced emotional connections.

We are a direct combination of biology and chemistry: a biological body, with dominant genes of our inherited genetic code then altered by a unique combination of chemical interactivity caused by the release of hormones interacting with the genetic sequences of our individual self. While we recognize our physical sensory input today, we should know that our spiritual connectivity can also provide input that may be misinterpreted as the same sensory input we've always known. This spiritual connection is critical to understand, and potentially manage, to better understand what we think we know, as it affects everything processed by the human brain to become our knowledge. While we are certainly a product of our ancestry, we are just as much the product of the interpretation of the spiritual environment we evolve through. Ultimately, we seek emotional intellect and empathy. When our physical body fails, we are left with our memories to assist others still here on the physical plane.

Being in a physical form takes time to master, and some will only reach the average usage of the biological body throughout the time given on earth. The fact that the bonding between the physical and spiritual selves happens soon after conception gives our spiritual self the opportunity to assist in the arrangements of the genetic construction by alternatively selecting a recessive gene instead of the dominant one as one example. It also fosters a channel of communications between the physical and spiritual selves by including the spiritual self in the construction of said biological pieces of the newly created physical entity.

Once the physical entity draws air for the first time, it really becomes a "training wheels off" type of function where the spiritual entity needs to begin the task of arranging the body functions, as well as the sensory input. It's not easy at first; however, things get easier as the two entities begin to function as one. This process has repeated itself trillions of times throughout the existence of life, and so the journey truly begins to experience the rollercoaster of emotional interaction.

Understanding the implications and ramifications of our physical self, understanding how the physical self came to the time and space that we find ourselves in, is as equally important as knowing our spirituality. Our biological body will provide additional manipulations to the incoming sensory input, which will be both the physical senses and the spiritual connections. Therefore, it is just as important to know what you are as it is to know who you are.

With all this understanding and controlling of the emotional stability within our new physical form, emotional control becomes necessary to obtain and maintain for our successful lessons here on the physical plane. This brings us to obtaining a better control and constant expansion of our emotional intellect.

What About Us Specifically?

From a physiological perspective, you are created from the spiritual influence placed upon the genetic structures offered by your parents. As these two genetic constructs are placed together, the process of determining which dominant and submissive gene becomes prominent, I believe is done by your spiritual self, based on the lessons you wish to learn. Each part of the construct that you start with determines a path you will take throughout your physical life. Whether it be eye color, hair color, skin color, heavy-set or thin, male, female, or intrinsic thought construction, this original genetic construct outlines the lessons you hope to achieve in this lifetime. From this genetic construct comes the release of specific quantities of different hormones within the bloodstream, thereby creating what our brain interprets as emotions. All these chemical interactions cause the brain to interpret physical sensory input differently, thereby creating a different stored memory and relational links between those memories.

EXERCISES

Chapter 2: Seeking Answers From The Previous Chapter

In the previous section, we highlighted a few of the questions you can fully deliberate to determine where in your journey of enlightenment you are, as well as determining our current trajectory in this physical existence. As with the entirety of life within the planes of existence, we find that all things are intertwined and in a never-ending circle of understanding. Let us evaluate the questions to determine what we can glean from them; I'll use my answers as an example.

1. **What is your personal defined difference between spirituality and religion, or are they the same?**

    My understanding is that religion was/is merely a form of population control; we know that there was/is a sliver of spirituality in the major religions of the world. However, it's clear that the millennia of misinformation and population manipulation that has occurred in conjunction with these religions would dictate that many of its followers are purely following by rote or by fear. In many cases, I have personally seen where the application of practice is more important than the spiritual connections necessary to fully understand. It is for this reason that I have written this book. Spirituality to me defines the connection that we all have with the past, present, and future of any form that contains the universal life force, or "life". Human or not, the universe that we recognize is all part of the physical plane, and those entities who have chosen to assume the form of a different type are just as connected as we are. In addition, our past (ancestors), our present (others around us), and our future (descendants) all possess a spiritual connection with us all the time. Religion is an exercise I do to demonstrate my beliefs and not the belief itself.

2. **Does being a non-believer of religion disconnect you from spirituality?**

    Quite the contrary. In some cases, non-believers of a practice are less limited by the influence of those practices and can experience more of the world that believers cannot, due to the intentional closing of the possibilities within their own minds. Throughout the existence of religious practices, a major thread of "label making" has been employed and fervently attached to everything. This need to apply labels to everything was put into place by those who needed to feel superior to others, whereas we know that most things in this universe are without a firm definition or label. This application of labels has led to further misinterpretation and misunderstanding of natural differences between the many different energy alignments being offered by the universe to our minds. Our spiritual connection to our ancestors, as well as other life forms who share this physical existence, is a constant. Like the heartbeat, or the breath, it comes in the form of energy that we can interpret with our physical sensory input. Sometimes it we must detach from the societal influences for a while, particularly from a paradigm designed to quash individuality and freedom of thought.

3. **What does spirituality mean to you? Is it a doctrine (Christian, Muslim, Buddhists, etc.) associated with a church somewhere? Is it a natural part of life with or without humankind?**

   In my humble opinion, spirituality is not a doctrine, but the breathing of the physical existence. As the two planes of existence (physical, spiritual) overlap and intersect, the entities on those two planes are almost forced to interact at some level. Many people I've interacted with over the years are quick to discount the other forms of life on this physical plane. If it is not human, it bears no value to their spirituality, which could be no further from the truth. Every blade of grass has a level of life within it, therefore produces a spiritual energy that it can send out. The mountains, the trees, every living thing sends energy and can foster the communications with ancestors and descendants. As defined later, each of us possess a spiritual entity within us who resides on the spiritual plane, and when your spiritual self connects deeply with your physical self, this is where spirituality really begins. Each life on this plane possesses both entities, therefore spirituality is when I am using the spiritual self to explore the worlds around me.

4. **If you say you are having a "spiritual experience", what does that mean to you?**

   For me, having a spiritual experience means that I am breathing. It means that I am seeing, hearing, tasting, smelling, and feeling the physical world around me and transferring that knowledge and experience to my spiritual self. Because I have come to understand that I will need these experiences once my biological body ceases to communicate with my descendants and ancestors (as I do now), without the influence of my physical sensory input or the chemical interactivity of emotions, I know that every part of living is a lesson learned. By recognizing the end-goal of having experiences to relay to my descendants, I am preparing myself to move outside of my physical body. Spirituality is all around us every second of every day. Realizing that concept has made my whole existence a spiritual one.

5. **Do you explore spirituality by yourself? Does anyone else have to be present for you to experience your definition of spirituality?**

   One is never alone when realizing the spiritual realm intersects with the physical one, everywhere, all the time. However, the physical plane of existence is the only place where the concept of time and space occurs. Because the physical limitations of time and space have been so embedded in our thought process, many struggle to understand the idea of communicating with our ancestors or our descendants. Too many times we place limitations or barriers in the communications we may receive because our ancestor lived so long ago, or we haven't even found a mate yet for descendants. I understand that I lived in spiritual form long before I accepted the physical one, and while others may believe that they experienced the physical realm before in another form, the underlying concept of "duality" which is where I am both a spiritual being and a physical one at the same time is a known. This means I am never alone. Do I need other physical entities to occupy the same space or belief path with me? No.

6. **What is the value of your definition of a god?**

   In much the same way I use my totems, or amulets, I use a defined idea of a god to direct energy to and from. Where I recognize that there are two distinct states of energy that I receive, the masculine and the feminine, both equally important in managing my mental clarity along my journey of life. Because I recognize that the energy being sent by my definition of a god is all around me every day, I direct my requests (prayers, magic spells) to a specific label of this definition of a god. I have chosen to use the names my ancestors did as a sign of respect for their ways.

7. **How do we recognize the influence of our ancestors?**

   Recognizing the influence of our ancestors is accomplished by looking in the mirror each morning. While I have never seen them face-to-face on the physical realm, I have become intimately familiar with them and can therefore communicate with them by speaking to the entity in the mirror. Whether we are directly tied to a particular social group from antiquity or not is moot, as ancestors from many cultures may interact with us on certain levels

Absorbing the Energy of This Knowledge

Throughout this section, we have explored the incredibly unique individual you are. We discussed the evolution of humankind, psychology, and theology; however, those are merely influences in who we are personally. This section's exercises are a little more challenging, as we discover what emotional landmines you have placed in your mind. As we discussed throughout the chapter, your genetic construction, balanced against the chemical composition, creates distinct communication channels for you to receive information about the different worlds around you. A couple of emotional triggers seem to be more excitable than others, but why? The control of your spiritual communication relies heavily on our emotional control. With that in mind, let us explore some of those thoughts that make us, us. Remember, make notes about your answers here, then compare your answers to the thoughts following the meditation section.

1. My deepest fear is what? Why?
2. My greatest joy is what? Why?
3. What do you believe about a "god"? How much were you taught, or how much "occurred to you"?
4. What did my mother's genetics give me? My father's?
5. How is my body physiologically different from anyone else's?
6. If I could, I'd love to speak to my 2nd great grandmother. What would you say? Why?
7. What does my grandchild think of my contribution to the family?

Visualize the reality of how special you are. Many have told me that they can't find anything unique about themselves; however, by virtue of the genetic modification throughout the millennia, there is no way your genetics will identically match any other existence on either plane. This is just one of the many things that makes you incredibly unique. Understanding how you are you allows you to establish a baseline as to why your ancestors chose the path they did. In addition, this provides common ground for you to establish communications with your ancestors and descendants going into the future.

Adopting the Successful Wisdom Using Meditation

To thoroughly comprehend the wisdom and knowledge passed to us from the elders and ancestors, we must embed the new information deep within our psyche to determine when the data received meets the necessary burden of proof for our heart and our mind in concert. An exercise that can assist with this is the art of meditation.

Like we did in the last chapter, we are going to meditate on the questions we've asked above and make notes of the responses we receive. Here we discover many of the boundaries that we have established within our mind, limiting our expansion into the spiritual universe that intersects with our physical one. Our meditation topic is going to delve into what makes us think and act the way we do. By understanding the gifts and limitations placed on us by the genetic transference from our ancestry, we can begin to understand how we can grow through and with it.

Unfortunately, this section is where many people struggle when they discover an emotional memory that causes great discomfort, and they stop. Not wanting to endure the pain. It is through the slow unraveling of these memories that we can begin to find the peace we seek. However, be cautious that you do not take on too much. Instead of addressing the emotional memory, ask yourself why you have this type of reaction. In some cases, people discover that they have been wronged by another entity on this plane, and while this may be true, why should we carry their guilt? Of which they have none?

Each meditation session should be enlightening as you find memories whose emotional association does not hold power over you anymore and can be discarded. In life, I am convinced that we will find what we seek. If we choose to find and carry negative memories, they will deteriorate our spiritual bonding. On the other side of the coin, should we choose to drop memories that only contain negativity, we begin our journey of true enlightenment.

Chapter Three

Before I venture into our emotional intelligence, I need to be sure I inform you that my presentation here is based on a layman's understanding. While I have worked with thousands of individuals, paying close attention to the many symptoms that these individuals face, you will only find very limited scientific or medical phrases in this section. The Landvætti have had a very powerful hand in explaining these concepts to me.

Success on the physical plane of existence is based on the emotional intellect we acquire to become empathetic toward other entities, regardless of their plane of existence. When considering what is meant by emotional control, we must consider a concept of being without sight, sound, or any other physical sensory input, nor the physical chemicals required for emotional manipulation, yet retaining the ability to communicate with entities on multiple planes. This communication is created by the empath being able to sense a need from another. Whether the need is physical or intellectual, being able to establish the required level of empathy is the lesson that the physical plane offers.

Consider the self, or our consciousness, as a "black box". Our memories and knowledge bits are stored inside this box. When our mind is created during our conception, it is empty. Our life experiences fill the box throughout our lifetime. However, the only way to get those memories and knowledge bits into the box is through five attached hoses. Those hoses are our physical senses (vision, hearing, smell, taste, touch). There is no other way into the box. Without these five hoses, our mind continues to be empty. If one of the hoses gets damaged, we have seen within the medical community where other hoses will enlarge to provide some of the missing data. This is the condition that we, as humans, find ourselves. Because emotional control is primarily driven by our sensory input, we understand that we seek the ability to control our interpretation of our senses.

Throughout our existence on the physical plane, we need to understand the power of the chemical interaction that we interpret as emotions, as they alter, at a fundamental level, the actual knowledge we think we have. With the combinations of genetic engineering and chemical interactions from the sensory input that is passed to the brain, we interpret the experiences with our surroundings to form knowledge and wisdom, and most importantly, emotional memories.

When discussing emotional intelligence, we need to understand several facets about emotional intellect.
1. What are emotions from a scientific view?
2. Why are emotions so important?
3. What is emotional control?

Scientifically

Again, by no means do I want you to consider my knowledge within the biological chemistry as an authoritative source of this specialty, as I merely interpret what I am taught by the spiritual entities of the Landvætti, in addition to my theorizing throughout the decades of working with many individuals. I would encourage you to do your own reading or confirm with your medical provider; however, I believe it's critical to have a general understanding as to how the (particularly human) biochemistry works.

To begin this conversation in earnest, we must understand how our body creates emotions. Our biological body uses hormones to alter the chemical state of the body. A hormone is defined as:

> *"Hormones are your body's chemical messengers. They travel in your bloodstream to tissues or organs to help them complete what is necessary to do. They can work slowly, over time, and affect many different processes to include growth and development, metabolism which allows your body to gain physical form and energy from the foods you eat. Some hormones may seemingly affect the mood (or feelings) of an individual much more quickly, such as adrenaline."*
> —Alaska Úlfheðnar

A significant number of hormones within the human body may cause additional hormones to be released. When these hormones are released into the bloodstream and mixed with those already in the bloodstream, it affects the pH balance of the chemistry directly surrounding the neural pathways, the spinal cord, and the brain. This alteration filters any data that is passed down these paths to the brain by either our physical sensory input or by our imagination, as both are very capable of initializing the process of hormone release.

The body uses many hormones to regulate the mood, or mental state, of the individual. Many of these hormones are released by the surrounding muscles of the heart and have a spectrum as to how much is released, or not released, as well as any potential counteragents already in the bloodstream. In most cases, our biological bodies can release counteragents that nullify the effect of the hormone if determined necessary.

Let's look at just a few of the hormones of the human physiology.

- Adrenaline is our "go drug" used during excitement. This hormone is released by the adrenal glands within the medulla portion of the brain. Triggered by the "fight or flight" reaction identified within the amygdala portion of the brain stem, which interprets the signals received from the multiple physical sensory input received. Essentially, adrenaline is the hormone that prepares the biological body for survival in a stressful situation. This is one of the conditions where we can see the manipulation of other sensory inputs, as adrenaline decreases the brain's ability to interpret other input signals sent via the central nervous system, such as pain. This hormone causes several manipulations to the brain and body, which may alter the sensory input data, thereby storing corrupted data bits as knowledge within the memory of the brain. (Example: a traumatic event may be stored as corrupted data bits, either visual or auditory bits that can be interpreted very differently depending on the other chemicals within the bloodstream at the time.)

- Cortisol is one of the many steroid hormones, again produced in the adrenal glands within the medulla of the brain; however, it is additionally controlled by the hypothalamus and the pituitary gland. The benefit of cortisol is that most cells of the body have cortisol receptors, thereby able to quickly accept the effects of cortisol. Another one of our stress hormones, it controls blood sugars and regulates metabolism, as well as many other functions within the biological body.
- Dopamine is responsible for our "happy" feelings.
- Melatonin is the body's way of getting ready for sleep as it promotes a cycle of sleep and wakefulness, as higher levels are found toward the sleep time at night. This hormone performs many functions throughout the body, particularly based around seasonal biology. Mixed messages sent using this hormone may alter sensory input based on this seasonal rotation, as we find many times when individuals are removed from their seasonal divisions, such as moving from Minnesota to Florida, minimizing the differences between the seasons under the Florida heat. In much the same way the other hormones affect us, so too does this one.
- Serotonin is the major player in altering our baseline psychology as its effects can be felt across the gamut of neural connectivity of the body. Serotonin is the primary hormone that stabilizes

our mood and feelings of well-being, as well as happiness. When our intrinsic levels of serotonin are low, we experience a sense of depression. In contrast, when they are high, we can be irritable and fidgety. This is a powerful player in the world of our intrinsic genetic chemistry, as it impacts many processes.
- Oxytocin is typically a social hormone and connects a mommy to a baby. In men, however, it affects the production of testosterone, which we know has a great impact on the thought process. Just another consideration to think about when attempting to understand the biological unit we inhabit.
- Acetylcholine is used to help us learn and memorize.
- Norepinephrine, when we see lower counts, results in depression. This would be a counteragent to the adrenaline release, helping to restore calmness.

Each of these hormones, when released into the bloodstream, influence the way we are capable of thinking, and, more importantly, processing sensory input to produce stored memories or knowledge. Within the general order of things, these hormones obtain a baseline balance where your biological body learns to operate. There has never been, nor will there ever be, a state within the biological body referred to as normal. It merely becomes your individual and unique baseline of behavior built around your unique combination of chemical interactivity within your genetic structure.

This is a critical factor to understand: no one is normal.

We are our own unique version of normal. We are all just a little different from a chemical, as well as genetic, perspective. Therefore, another critical concept here is that, as we change our emotional baseline, our brain simply adjusts for the changes, establishing a new version of normal. This is where we find that some among us seem more content to be under a substantial amount of stress, where others seem to implode.

Because of our genetic gifts from our parents, this chemical composition will be completely different for each of us. This then sets up the argument of a group parallel to an identical emotional understanding to be technically, fundamentally, impossible. This is a very short list of potential chemical alterations but needs to be seriously considered when attempting to wrap our mind around the miniature changes within our chemical composition that may affect what our sensory input provides. The major two considerations here are:

1.) Our entire understanding of "emotion" is based on what our biological chemistry is doing at any one moment, thereby affecting how we see the world.

2.) Things can change in an instant. As our body releases hormones into an already higher potential baseline of chemistry in the bloodstream, it can cause a higher level of confusion about describing this "feeling".

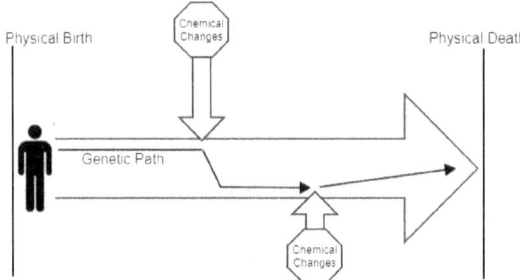

Figure 10 - *Alteration of the genetic structure by the emotional state changes.*

Some hormones quash stress by being released following a particular rush for either physical or intellectual charges. There are over 50 neuromodulators that our body uses to manipulate how we are feeling at any given time. When considering the list above, we need to consider a possibility of mixing many of them together during a particular event. Scientifically (or medically) speaking, emotional intellect is really bringing the heart and limbic system into synchronization with each other to control what is released and when. Because of the microscopic tolerances of these recognized chemical changes, a small change in the pH balance can create a substantial emotional change by the individual.

All these chemical reactions happening within the body during an experience with emotion that can thereby alter the bodies' fundamental structure at the genetic level. This modification of the genome is then passed on to future generations. We are conceived with a snapshot of that moment in time of the genetic structure of our parents. As we age, our chemical interactions begin to further manipulate our genetic structure, continuing the cycle of constant emotional evolution. We will discuss in a minute about attempting to control this whole process.

The challenge with this is that for us to be fully embrace success in our endeavor here on the physical plane, we must seek and find a sustainable balance of the influences of these hormone swings. Our goal is to be able to consciously release counteragents, if necessary, to bring our chemical balance back under our emotional control, constantly refining our ability to manage the pH balances of our physical self.

Chemical Control of Psychology

Because of our foundational genetic construct interacting with our sometimes volatile chemical composition, and our perceived knowledge base being prone to these potential psychological manipulations of previous sensory input, we should always be suspect of what we think we know.

The chemical interactions happening within the body can discard sensory input, and things like pain can be rejected all together. This concept of chemical interference with sensory input brings to the forefront then, the idea that, in the same way, our spiritual interactivity happening all the time could have similar results. When our spiritual entities are communicating to or through us, and if something presented provokes a memory bit with some emotion related to it, the body's chemistry is then altered, thereby any other data received afterwards by the brain should become suspect.

Whether discussing concepts like blind rage or painless sex, even the idea of running for miles with a severe injury to escape something, the chemistry blocking other sensory input has been a part of the understanding of emotions. The significance here is that in much the same way these chemical compositions can completely alter what we experience with our five senses and create corrupted or missing "memories" within the mind, we find that spiritual interactions may fall victim to the same process. In most cases, the idea of another spiritual entity being released from the physical vessel is very traumatizing and can alter all our sensory input, causing us to question the things we think we know.

I hope I've given you enough information to question everything you think you know. By addressing the potential corruption within the mind, you have a strong foundation in which to form future knowledge and wisdom in its place. By challenging or replacing these memory bits, we are constructing a mind of truth, minimizing the added stress of monitoring as closely as possible facts arriving from our sensory input. More importantly, hopefully I've revealed the importance of understanding how our emotions can create false narratives within our mind that then become the foundation in which we structure additional knowledge on. This is my hope, anyway. By understanding this, we can better prepare ourselves by shifting our focus to harmony and peaceful joy, allowing the sensory input to see the better things within this physical lifetime. By keeping our mind focused on the good things, we can then be more attentive to those things, making all things a little better. While this may sound quite "cheeky", the reality is, the more inner joy we conjure up, the better able we are able to minimize corrupt memory.

Emotional Control

As we discussed in a previous section, emotions are simply a chemical reaction between released hormones within the body and the underlying genetics given by our ancestry, ultimately surrounding the neural pathways and interpreted by the brain. Primarily, we need to monitor our heart, as most of the hormone releases happen in muscles near the heart into our bloodstream. This immediate reaction is caused by the sensory input traveling up the neural pathway through the brain stem into places like the amygdala and hypothalamus, which then signal the release of stimulant agents into our bloodstream, if necessary, automatically, without conscious interaction from us. This means that we need to have our "flight or fight" process clearly defined, that are programmed into all parts of the chain of interactions necessary for bringing the signals to the hypothalamus, as well as the pituitary and adrenal glands within the brain, thereby initiating our instinctual response.

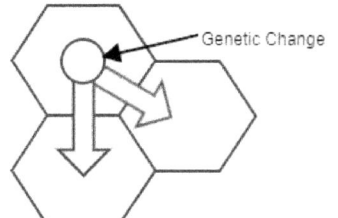

Figure 11 - *By manipulating a cell with our emotional chemistry, the process of cellular splitting carries the change.*

The added challenge is that we are all unique in that we initially duplicate our parents' genome structure at the moment of our conception; however, after birth, our chemical composition begins the process of altering our genetic sequence throughout our physical lifetime. We know that there are some cases where the recessive gene is selected over the dominant one. I believe that this is the moment where our spiritual selves are introduced to our physical self, and some alteration is provided by this spiritual entity. In addition, we know that our ancestors have passed on some of their universal genetics through our parents, adding additional construct differences, making us incredibly unique. This passing on of the genetic structure has two forms. They are either dominant or recessive or, in some rare cases, neither, thereby introducing a random genetic anomaly. Another theory would be that our deity determines whether the dominant genetic expression will trump the recessive one or the other way around. This decision is made during the instant of conception. The genetic structure will navigate through 3 billion bases, or 20,000 genes on 23 pairs of chromosomes[1], to isolate and determine the outcome of where we begin life. Many of

1   https://www.genome.gov/about-genomics/fact-sheets/Deoxyribonucleic-Acid-Fact-Sheet

these genes represent how our biological body will manage the release of hormones as well as other chemistry alterations and ultimately work as the undercarriage for emotions.

This, then becomes the biological lessons that we must seek to master, which allow us to retain a better collection of memories and knowledge. We spend our physical lifetime learning how to control the release of hormones, thereby controlling the emotional reactions we experience. There are always different and unique situations we find ourselves in that require a different level of control, and on some rare occasions may not be enough (what may not be enough?). However, there are always different ways we can consider putting the necessary checks and balances within our brain that can arrest the emotional rush to retain control.

We need to establish a baseline for our emotional state. These baselines are times where we are very familiar with our emotional states and are in control of things that might affect it. Many have chosen to use meditation exercises for baselining our emotional states, and this can provide a wonderful support for our guided meditations to discover the expanse of our own mind. The idea is to obtain a level of emotional neutrality where you can assess what is affecting you and determine the best path forward in controlling it in the future.

What would a discussion about our emotional control be without addressing the two powerhouses: love and fear. In a very separate way, our brain uses our multiple paths of sensory input to validate a perceived need to be scared or elated. Love and fear are different. These two emotional conditions do not need sensory validation; one is a natural state, the other a display by the ego. It doesn't take a brain surgeon to figure out which is which. As we've discussed previously, the brain can be fooled into believing these states exist by altering our intrinsic chemistry, using either illegal or legal chemicals. However, when identifying them in a natural state, we know that love is an openness and acceptance and is a natural, pure energy provided to us from Mother Earth.

Love is the most powerful of emotions, followed by its opposite: fear. Typically, we express the deepest levels of anger toward those we love the most. Why? This really comes down to the chemical hurricane going on in the neural pathways debilitating our sensory input, as well as most rational thought. Love can expose us and make us feel vulnerable and weak, yet it can also fill our hearts and exponentially multiply our strength and perseverance. The chemicals involved with love can also produce extrinsic symptoms like irregular heartbeats, perspiration, or change in breathing patterns. Ultimately, it is no different from engaging the fight-or-flight system.

Love is power.

Fear, on the other hand, is an emotional response typically engaged by the ego when it manifests some evidence of being slighted or hurt, a retaliatory action. Fear is the ego's way of dealing with any ideas and input it doesn't understand and is therefore unable to process within the brain. This is typically engaged by another part of the brain stem called the amygdala, or the "Flight or Fight" processing center. Fear can have a multitude of demonstrated paths. The first is that of retreat and attempt to recover balance. Whether that is escaping a situation to regroup one's thoughts and actions necessary to continue or shutting down emotionally until balance can be restored. The other path includes the chemical reduction of love and compassion to expose the anger that lies beneath. Depending on the level of reduction of calming hormones, this state can cause the loss of other sensory input. Anger is not nearly as powerful as its counteragent and can immediately be deflated by love.

Love is one of the chemical compositions that emulates the natural frequency of the earth. When considering the projection of our personal aura, the influence of love slows the frequency to become more aligned with the earth, which is why we may have different feelings when visiting points in nature or being near loved ones. Mother Earth is constantly emanating the frequency and energy of love in every direction, all the time.

When considering how we feel, we must carefully evaluate all the potential influences we could be experiencing at any given time. The auras of mankind have become one of "win at any cost" and many have surrendered their intrinsic honor for material gains, not realizing or knowing that this surrender has undermined their chances of life's ultimate success. This mentality is then projected onto others, thereby conflicting with the natural energies from Mother Earth and our other spiritual entities, in most cases causing conflicts within the hearts of the remainder of humankind. Aura interactions create energy. This energy is then interpreted by the neural pathways for the appropriate emotional releases, which then can create a narrative in the mind that their path is the correct one.

I will state for the record, it is not. All the money in the world cannot heal the sick, cannot win a heart, nor can it prevent the heart from breaking. It is only a materialistic convenience for our physical lifespan. Love can do all these things. Our real wealth lies in the emotional chaos called love.

Noble Virtues

Going back into antiquity to the study of my ancestry, we discover that not only did the Vikings live by a strict warrior code (contrary to most beliefs), but this same code has also been adopted again and again by groups throughout history. This is important because not only should we seriously consider these virtues within our community but intrinsically as well. We will struggle to see true success until we are honest with ourselves and hold ourselves accountable for the emotional control necessary.

In the days of the Norse, before the times of those from Scandinavia, many individuals followed a personal pursuit of nine noble virtues:

1. Honor includes everything from doing what was right by one's family definition to subscribing to integrity in

every interaction. The term honorable can be applied to both participants of a great battle or farmers who tended the fields even when they may not have wanted to. While many may have transposed the principle of honor with the idea of glory, the fact that those who are not "stacking bodies" could live honorably is the reality.

2. Truth is where the idea of integrity comes into the required virtues of our ancestors. Truth is about being absolutely truthful, regardless of whether someone is watching or not. Some in modern times struggle with this, as it is one of the first virtues surrendered in exchange for an abused self-esteem. Being truthful about our feelings is another area we struggle with, as this leads to a feeling of vulnerability that many fear.

3. Courage is the ability to face our fears. It includes fears of exposing our deepest feelings, and many have sought ways around the lack of individual courage by supplementing extrinsic avoidance techniques (i.e., drinking liquid courage, etc.) whereas this is simply the removal of inhibition, allowing the inner personality to be visible.

4. Fidelity is a form of honor and a portion of truth. However, when one alters the view of one's oath to another (such as being married), one quickly discovers the honor and truth portions of this oath. Therefore, when considering one's fidelity to another person, maybe we should see it as a blood oath. In the beliefs of the Norse, oath breakers were the lowest form of life and condemned to the lowest bowels of the realm of Hel, to drown in a poisonous river of snake venom until Ragnarök.

5. Discipline is another core virtue that I think we've stepped away from as a society. To me, this means that we stay the course no matter the personal cost. Ultimately, it is our ability to carry out a specific task regardless of what our trajectories may introduce into our lives. Discipline is solidifying what one thinks and feels toward a particular task and getting it done.

6. Hospitality was the proof that one was comfortable with what one possessed. Whether it be with our material or intellectual

property, we offered it freely, knowing it would be cared for and returned in better condition than it was borrowed. However, I feel as if hospitality was a form of honor in that we would honor our guests with whatever we had.

7. Industriousness was what our ancestors did. They recognized the amount of labor necessary and went about the task of getting it done. They didn't seek ways around it and didn't avoid it. One might say that herein lay the steps to being honorable in one's life. By taking care of what needed to be done, they lived their lives honorably. This too should be a path for us as well. Being willing and able to do more than we are and keeping those things we need maintained are all part of living an honorable life.

8. Self-Reliance was probably my personally most admired virtue of my ancestors. While many of them would have had to carve out their existence from the frozen winter grounds, they never expected a handout from their deities or the spiritual entities. They knew what had to be done and they got it done. While many terms can be thrown in here, like "initiative" and "forward thinking," it all came down to not hoping for tasks to be completed but getting into their lives and getting it done.

9. Perseverance is another of my ancestor's virtues that I find is still applicable today. The ability to continue even when the physical realm is stacking up obstacles. Ultimately, this is another demonstrative value of honor. By not giving up, or giving in, even when everything around you says otherwise.

When considering our forward trajectory, we need to seriously consider these virtues, as I believe the modern monotheistic practices attempted to force them upon the population of the time with some of the practices aimed at guiding individuals to living an honorable life. Of course, their version of honor became misconstrued with the term glory, which is very different.

When the topic comes up about "what's different between then and now," these are the subjects I discuss. These are the different mindsets that our ancestors had before the days of public assistance. I believe these are some of the virtues that we can take away that will ultimately make our lives more simplistic and easier to gain more control of our emotional state.

Just as importantly is the idea that my ancestors *lived*. They lived intentionally. They did the necessary tasks. They wanted to do those tasks or understood they needed to be done. They didn't seek out magicians to do it for them, they knew they had to make their own way. This idea of living intentionally has faded, with many simply waiting for someone else to complete a task. My ancestors wanted to do all the things necessary to ensure their lives succeeded and didn't wait until the gods showed some type of favor. They just did it.

Personal Judgment

Earlier, we discussed the psychology of what makes us think and act the way we do. However, we would be negligent if we didn't address the psychological impact of the perceived necessity of segregation imposed by many in this day and age, which created a level of distinction between themselves and others by including the "we versus them", or "have and have nots" mentality encouraged by the early architects of these religious practices in an effort to further the influence these new practices would need to elevate themselves.

The evangelical branches of these practices weaponized this perceived need to enforce judgment on individuals who would not conform to the whim of the church leadership of the time and place. These practices condemned thousands to die unnecessarily to ensure that the message of "conform or die" was received in the recesses beyond the immediate visibility of the central church. This form of understanding is purely intertwined with the monotheistic practices, which would ultimately drive subscription to the practice in fear.

We also discover the deliberate perception and further development of a sense of superiority. While strength and IQ are impressive traits, the ultimate victory goes to those who are willing and able to find others who need and provide help. However, from a physical entity perspective, no singular entity is superior to another. All life forms on the physical plane are equal in every necessary way to each other. Upon departure from the physical plane, we are all formless and have no need for those things left behind, especially our physical form. Superficial value judgments and superiority complexes are simply a weakened spirit attempting to deploy a damaged ego.

We need to recognize that inferiority creates inadvertent agents of dispersal for these new practices of minimizing others to compensate for their perceived inferiority. Furthermore, I believe some bravado is put into place because of an entity's inability to recognize the wondrous collection of moving pieces, resulting in a reduced level of self-worth. Embracing our uniqueness is what creates the different perspectives that are so important and add so much to the overall picture of existence.

Uniqueness of the Individual

As we have learned about the genetic composition that is given at conception, followed by a physical lifetime of modifications to our genetic structure caused by the chemical interactions occurring naturally within our biology, I believe we can all begin to perceive the uniqueness that is the self. This should lead us to understand the incredible challenge that each of us faces when attempting to understand the influence that the biological interactivity has on our intelligence and stored knowledge. This becomes our baseline in understanding how the potential corruption of stored knowledge can alter our reaction to sensory experiences happening around us.

This uniqueness is also present in our relationship with whatever force we decide to refer to as a deity or spiritual entities. In the same way that the incredibly volatile chemical composition within us dictates our physical interactions, so too does it determine the alignment with our spiritual entities. This unique combination of hormones within the bloodstream interacting with the genetic structure or our individuality creates an incredibly unique relationship with our understandings of spirituality. Before we attempt to sign on with a mass understanding of an organized religious practice, I hope that we take into consideration our incredibly unique relationship with the spiritual realm around us and especially our understanding of the intimate relationship with our deity figure.

On the same page is the idea as to how special we each are. Being able to see a problem from a different perspective is what makes us each valuable to the solution. By implementing our unique collection of knowledge gained through our chemical and genetic processes, we offer a unique perspective that should be embraced as part of the larger image of a situation or condition.

Our Ego

In many of the works of Sigmund Freud (1856-1939), he explained his understanding of our ego as an interpretation of our perceived reality within the subconscious human mind. In most cases, this was superseded by the super ego, which was based on our understanding of morality. His interpretation of our super ego that spanned both the subconscious and unconscious minds placed a substantial burden on our unique perception of value in some form of morality.

I believe that this ego is enlisted in our adult lives as a protection mechanism. Our ego will alter receiving data from the physical sensory input based on our individual perception of the self, potentially fooling ourselves into the belief that reality is different from how it really is. As a protection mechanism, this produces behaviors of pride or bravado which can be seen as necessary for reducing negative impacts to our emotionally charged memories.

One of the single largest challenges we have as spiritual beings is the lessons of learning to control one's ego, as it can be very fragile yet domineering at times, and it can have a substantial amount of influence over the chemical release within the human body. However, like all things in nature, one's ego must be maintained within certain limits. Too much and one misses the lessons we are here to learn, while too low and you spend more time attempting to elevate the self-worth and less time learning to explore your spirituality. Within the boundaries of chemical balance, the ego plays a part in releasing certain hormones, which may trigger others, thereby reducing the physical sensory ability to listen to what others may be attempting to communicate. We all have plenty of experiences where those who exhibit symptoms of an over-inflated ego are completely unable to hear or process what we are saying to them.

Our ego is created by the mind as a representation of what we think we are to other people, but primarily it is a defense mechanism to protect our inner emotional control center.

An interesting piece to know is that only other spiritual entities can see, or care to see, another's ego, as an extrinsic display of the ego is called bravado. In most cases, because our raw emotional state is projected through our aura, most spiritual entities will jump in to help because they can see through the bravado put on for show and recognize the need (or vacuum) within the individual's mind. However, an ego does have a function and can provide a great benefit for another subprocess: self-esteem and self-worth. In modern times, maintaining one's self-esteem is a full-time occupation, as there are a multitude of factors designed to break it down. Like all the other parts of the human thought process, ego needs to be controlled, and it's a part of the overall emotional control that we seek during our lifetime.

Our ego has a role to play within the realm of spirituality, too. By understanding its resistance to emotional surrender, we are given a tool to put the appropriate checks and balances in place that allow our conscious mind to arrest certain thought processes minimizing the emotional involvement. Think of this process as a doorway we pass through. Sometimes we can become disorientated on either side. When we begin our circular path outside this door, we refer to that as bravado, and it minimizes our potential for spiritual connectivity. When we are in a circular path behind the door, we become introverted and may struggle in connecting physically to our environment.

Learning to work with our ego is one task that *must* be accomplished prior to experiencing the true expanse of spirituality. While the defensive posture the ego takes needs to be enforced as to the limits it has, we do not want the ego crushing an opportunity to have a spiritual event just because someone else is watching (i.e., judging). You could inadvertently sever a relationship with a spiritual entity before it ever got started. Being mindful of our ego and ensuring it is under the same emotional control as the remainder of our emotions is critical to our success.

Empathy

Ah yes, that moment in time that it all comes together when we feel the emotional charge of another person: empathy. This journey of understanding the impact of the chemical disaster that happens in our bloodstream with some change in the environment. Empathy is our ability to extend our personal aura, with clarity, to discover the aura of another physical being, to receive and understand the chemical imbalance going on within their physical selves. It is done with the power of love. Having enough love to extend to another allows the empath to have the ability to look across auras.

However, just because we can intrinsically see across the auras does not mean that we'll be successful in translating what we see. This is where our emotional intellect comes in. By having had experiences throughout our physical existence where the chemical whirlwind produces a recognizable pattern, we are able to then translate the path forward to the individual. If we have never experienced a similar situation, then we must use generic steps to guide the individual back to safety within their mind. The best way to do this is to establish a baseline within their mental processing, then slowly step back toward the knowns within their minds. This is why it is important for us to have a varied experience base in which to help provide detailed steps as the path forward.

Throughout our physical lifetime, we will endure many types of emotional challenges that allow us to exercise our emotional control and perfect it. This lifetime experience provides us with two unique aspects of understanding because of our emotional control:

1. Our empathy to understand the emotional turmoil that is happening within others without having to rely on other sensory input to validate our findings. In other words, upon leaving our physical bodies behind after its demise, we must solely rely on our emotional empathy to locate individuals who need assistance in a similar experience to the ones we've had and determine a method in which to communicate with them.

2. By establishing a solid emotional control, we can minimize the corrupted data stored within our memories, hence our knowledge. This is a defined part of our intrinsic knowledge and wisdom we can offer to those who seek this. In much the same way we seek to find multiple reference points for data retained, we must seek to validate our sensory input.

Empathy is the ultimate accomplishment of the emotional educational journey that we spend a physical lifetime learning. While there are some among us who have already learned this ability, we (as humanity) need to focus on trying to be more like them. By consistently seeking harmony and co-existence and working to rid the world of negative judgments of all peoples, we minimize shame inflicted on others.

Being cognizant of the chemical effect on our biological genetic structure becomes paramount in guiding us to stabilizing our emotional controls and establishing a better connection to our spiritual self, as well as others, throughout the spiritual plane. For this reason, we need to understand, at least on a higher level, the impact of the chemical effect of emotions on our base DNA.

Summary

Understanding the emotional chaos within our body that affects every part of our knowledge, our aura, even our personality, is critical to understanding how we can interact with others who may be in a similar situation, mentally, and is critical to getting to a place in our lives where we can become empathetic. Empathy = love. This is why it is so important.

To gain clarity of the messages from our spiritual entities, as well as prepare to return to a spiritual realm where our physical sensory input and chemical blending is absent, we need to be able to obtain a level emotional state to produce a clear aura for communications.

EXERCISES

Chapter 3: Seeking Answers From The Previous Chapter

1. **My deepest fear is what? Why?**

   Many of us have deep-seated fears about something. Many times, this fear causes a volatile reaction within us that may seem out of character. In many cases, the ego is constructed to prevent something from getting to this irrational fear hidden down deep in our psyche. The answers you are looking for here are going to seem quite guttural in nature, as we uncover those hot memories that border on our deepest fear. However, ultimate emotional control would have us recognize the scenario before our ego does, thereby minimizing the influence the fear will have on our sensory input.

   My ancestors were vicious on the battlefield because they didn't fear death. While many of the modern population retain a natural fear of dying, in some cases, this fear of death prevents us from living to the fullest. That is not to say that they didn't enjoy life, they simply were not afraid of passing from this world to the next.

2. **My greatest joy is what? Why?**

   In much the same way fear is deep set, the avoidance of fear swings the pendulum in the other direction, allowing more of the "happy" chemicals to be released, thereby allowing our memories to be filled and associated with joy. Again, for the sake of emotional control, we just need to know what causes and what distracts from these major emotional volcanoes of the mind.

3. **What do you believe about a god? How much were you taught, or how much occurred to you?**

   Most of our physical existence is filled with people either purposefully, or not, filling our consciousness with thoughts about their idea of a deity. In addition, many of us are given more thoughts from television, literature, or the internet, about thousands of definitions of their god. They, most often, speak of methods to control others from the doctrine of their defined practice of religion. Is this where you got your ideas from, or have you had a personal relationship with a deity entity in another form?

4. **What did my mother's genetics give me? What about my father's?**

    Most often, when people discuss the idea of genetic transference, it is in reference to physical features (i.e., he has his mother's eyes or her father's nose). However, have you ever stopped to consider the conscious and unconscious behaviors that you exhibit both extrinsically and intrinsically? Have you ever said "...that's my father's thinking" when pondering one of life's challenges? Genetically, we get a substantial portion of our parents on our exterior, but we also get it all the way through. So, think about what line of thinking you have inherited, and is it still applicable to you and your environment?

    My father was an abusive alcoholic who was always scheming for a different way to make money. In addition, he struggled with accepting responsibility for the environment around him, taking extra effort to place blame for his learning opportunities on others. I broke this cycle, choosing a path of peace and acceptance. I'm not going to say "I'm cured" because I do retain an amount of passion about some things, and after-all, I am a Dane.

5. **How is my body physiologically different from anyone else's?**

    We've talked about the genetics and the chemistry involved in making you who you are, so hopefully this exercise brought to your attention the wonder of evolution that you are. You are truly special, and from a physiological standpoint, a one in one trillion.

6. **If I could, I'd love to speak to my 2nd Great Grandmother. What would you say? Why?**

    I do speak to both of my 2nd great grandmothers every day. They are two of my greatest supporters, but focusing on them deliberately, we can begin to form a connection with them and understand the connection from the other side.

7. **What does my grandchild think of my contribution to the family?**
   There is nothing in the world like my great-grandmother's sourdough bread! Or the many other pieces of our ancestry that came forward with each generation. This is why not only are we a genetic combination but a cultural extension of our ancestors. It is these types of memories that can be revered throughout your time. What will your grandchildren say about your contribution to these legacies?

Absorbing the Energy of This Knowledge

Contained within this chapter are the details about how you "feel" based on your genetics and the chemistry that interacts with those genes. Our focus should then be on our emotional stability, but I would recommend we practice some empathy. Empathy is challenging, I won't attempt to fool you, and we are going to add a level of complexity to our desire to learn empathy.

Remote empathy.

For our questions to ourselves, we are going to focus on someone who is outside your immediate surroundings. Maybe a friend who lives across town or family in another state. The idea is we will find them across the spiritual realm. I know what you're thinking, and I will tell you that you already do this more than you know. As an example, we'll use a friend across town whom we have visited (so we know what their home looks like). In our notes, we'll ask our questions to ourselves before we focus on them, then during meditation we'll see if the results are close. Afterwards there is a follow up portion.

First Step – Think of your friend and the last time you saw them. Picture their face temporarily. Just passing thoughts, really. Just to connect your mind to the aura.

1. What do you think they are doing right now?
2. How do you think they feeling right now?
3. What do you think are some of the things they are interacting with right now?
4. If you were there, what do you think they would say to you?

Again, we are simply reaching out with our minds into our aura for connectivity. Be sure to note the time you are making these thoughts, in addition to what you think you understand about any thoughts that "pop in" to your mind.

Adopting the Successful Wisdom Using Meditation

As you can imagine, empathy is a powerful tool to help us traverse large distances, even realms when necessary. It also closely connects us to others in a very deep way. Once we pass from our physical form, we use our skills of empathy to reach out to those still here to guide them on their journey. In addition, this is the method that we can use to communicate with our ancestors, whether here on the physical plane or not. As you may have noted above, I've used the term "think" in most of the questions. In our meditation, we are going to try to "see" the visions of what they are doing or thinking. This comes from a different level of focus and concentration. Remember that there will be a learning curve here, so don't criticize yourself. Like any skill, it takes practice.

In ancient times, men and women received visions. These visions were given to them by the ancestors to guide them on their life's journey. The skill of empathy has been employed for eons as a method of connectivity between those on the physical plane and those who are not. So, let us focus our meditation on seeking our friend.

As we close our eyes and concentrate, picture their face in our minds, maybe see them moving around. Draw forth your memories of them where you were together. As you get idea and thoughts or visions, be sure to make note of them, along with the time.

Finally, after spending time in meditation looking for them, contact them and see how you did. Remember, it's a skill that may take time to develop. Repeat this exercise often, expanding the search circles until you are reaching out to ancestors who left the physical plane thousands of years ago.

Chapter Four

Understanding Spirituality

We *will discuss the many* types of spiritual entities that inhabit this plane of existence with us, and we will also speak about how spiritual entities are created. But, in the worldwide view, what is this idea of spirituality? Many have tried to define it as love, others have said it is energy. The fact is, it is all that and much more. Through years of channeling spiritual entities, and then focusing more on the draw of wisdom using trance work, I have been able to ascertain how life throughout the spiritual plane manifests and is maintained. Let us gather as I retell the wisdom passed to me from the ancient ones, from those whom I call the Landvætti.

Before diving in too deep, let me say that these are facts that I have been given. While many of them have been hard for my finite mind to understand, the wisdom and knowledge that lies within the spiritual realm is endless.

In the process of creation, we know that particles of energy are released into the nothing outside the physical and spiritual planes. These microscopic particles coagulate into collections of energy in a continuous process of enhancing the energy contained within the mass. This mass, based on the amount of energy, obtains a consciousness and becomes self-aware. As it moves through this process, it is summoned via a vacuum created from the physical plane of a physical conception. The physical conception attracts this spiritual entity; however, we also know our spiritual self maintains its ability to exercise free will and can deny the vacuum created.

Spirituality in our Lives

So far, we have covered how our physical form arrived at this point in life, as well as understanding the incredibly unique genetic organism we are. Mostly during our discussion about the chemical storms that happen within our lives called emotions, we introduced the idea of these other forces at work within our physical lives that we need to understand. Hopefully, you took away the idea that there are two major threads to contend with when pondering the influence of spirituality:

1. Inbound spiritual interaction is where spiritual forces are suggesting information to us, via our aura, which is processed by the brain as physical sensory input, potentially altering what we think we know.
2. Outbound spiritual interaction is where we utilize our personal aura to reach out and communicate with other spiritual forces around us, usually in the forms of incanted spells or prayers.

Far beyond any practice is the sometimes elusive concept of our spirituality, to include what we'll call our theology, that we decide to subscribe to strictly based on our comfort and understanding. The first and most critical key is that every living thing is a spiritual creation at its core. Before we travel too far down the path of our discussion about spiritual understanding, I'd like to take a moment to define (for the sake of our discussion here) the basic concepts and terms I'll use:

- Spirituality, when used in a general context, is an umbrella statement that encompasses all spiritual interaction to include our personal theology, as well as the management of our communications with the spiritual entities around us. It can also demonstrate a state of mind that is obtained when we open our mind to the spiritual realm around us.
- Theology stems from our understanding of a deity and the interactions with that deity. Regardless of the count of deities, or what their names are, the idea that we recognize the need for, the power of, and the establishment of a deity form is our theology.
- Practice. The practice is the action(s) we use, and the action(s) required by the religious subscription. Whenever a theology includes an attempt to sway or convert others, this is indicative of a practice and no longer the theology.
- Religion is the combination of a theology and a practice. While some practices were developed as behavior control mechanisms, ultimately many have superseded the theology itself with the practice within these groups of religious organizations. Understanding why we act certain ways or do certain things is more important than just doing them.

We are spiritual entities who inhabit a physical body for the sole purpose of obtaining emotional experiences to master the art of empathy. Part of this existence within our spirituality is also a bi-directional connection channel between ourselves and the multitude of spiritual entities around us all the time, including a deity level collection of entities. To clarify the spiritual entities and their interaction with us, we need to better understand how this interaction may be visualized in our everyday lives. My personal history is an example of how these spiritual interactions can lead us to accept the education we need to succeed.

> When I was a young boy, like many, I too had "invisible friends" who would come and play with me when there was no one else. We played for hours uninterrupted, as they talked with me and introduced me to ideas and concepts of the knowledge base I would use later in my life. This initial introduction and

comfortability fostered my early childhood of imagination and growth in ways I now understand to be the gift it was. During these times, my mother had begun a study of the metaphysics and New Age understandings that had become popular during the early 1970s. As I paid attention, the things I heard her speak about seemed to make sense., and sometimes settled in my heart as knowledge and, ultimately, spiritual wisdom. My invisible friends nudged me during important lessons in her studies.

Many times, this is how the spiritual entities appear to young children who do not yet possess the ability, or the ego, to filter out their interactivity, nor the intrinsic chemistry to block their communication. They are invisible friends who can communicate effectively with an unfiltered mind and clear aura. Many of these early conversations lay the foundations for our potential extrapolations as new sensory data is received within the brain for the remainder of our physical existence. I believe that these conversations laid the groundwork for a future of maintaining relationships with spiritual entities who interact with me daily.

This early introduction to metaphysical beliefs was the first time that the Landvætti made themselves known to me and offered me the wisdom and knowledge that, I believe, set me on a trajectory of discoveries that threaded throughout my lifetime on the physical plane. During the 1970s and 1980s, my family traveled around the country extensively as my father was a licensed land surveyor and constantly chasing his fiscal dreams. Starting in western Ohio, to eastern Indiana, then back east to New Jersey, after a short stay in Pennsylvania. During these times, I remember having my "friends" who no one else could see spend time with me playing both inside the home and out.

In the summer of 1974, I relocated to Pierre Part, Louisiana, as my father surveyed the nuclear power plant construction in Taft, Louisiana. It was here that I was introduced to an overwhelming spiritual existence. Spending time playing on the levies that held in the mighty Mississippi river, I discovered a wealth of spiritual entities who visited with me, as well as my "friends". My time in Louisiana lasted until summer 1977, when we left for Tucson, Arizona, and another project of my fathers. Looking back, I admit the time in Louisiana left an indelible mark on my spiritual growth and understanding as I interacted with several priestesses of the practice or Vodou. These ladies introduced me to the other side, that spiritual realm beyond the eyesight of many.

Although many of the names and practices were different, their end goal was similar. The Vodou Priestesses I visited, and who visited me, were generous in their explanations as to their beliefs and their understandings. As a boy, I absorbed myself in understanding their practices and found myself on very comfortable ground as the Landvætti explained that they too sought to interact with the spiritual realm. Just as importantly, it was here that I began to uncover the similarities between the understandings of spirituality. The spiritual entities spoke to me, and it didn't seem to matter how I referred to them; they were open to our discussions.

> Our family arrived in Tucson in the summer of 1977, where I found a different group of spiritual entities who joined our everyday discussions, albeit by this time, the conversations had become more adult orientated. More deliberate in nature.

These spiritual entities were of the ancestry types, as they experienced emotional responses and understood my emotional turmoil of being the new kid in town. They explained the transitions, and I learned to respect the journey we all needed to engage. The lesson that I took from this portion of my spiritual journey was of the different types of spiritual entities, as well as their personal perspectives on issues that I faced in the modern day.

> I met a spiritual teacher and guide in the man who lived next to us in south Tucson. This teacher spoke of the spiritual world like it was across the street, like the entities he spoke to were physically with us, but he was much older than I was, which provided a legitimacy to my young mind. "White Sands" was a practicing medicine man of the Navajo tribe who lived in Tucson. I was afforded the opportunity to meet many of the

people who visited him and witnessed his ability to perform the natural healing he was capable of. I was entranced. These understandings and explanations he offered struck chords in my heart. They made absolute sense within my young mind, as well as seemingly fit perfectly with what my "invisible friends" had been speaking of for as long as I could remember at that point. This tutelage continued until girls, football, and fast cars began to preoccupy my teenaged mind, and we drifted apart.

This was the catalyst that sent me on a journey of understanding beyond my wildest imagination. While under the tutelage, I learned a lifetime of wisdom about the spiritual life forms who inhabit this plane of existence. Obviously in much the same way as most physical entities, my chemistry and genetics slowly began to change, further morphing myself in an attempt to meet a societal norm.

In the summer of 1980, my parents decided that they had grown apart and chose to divorce after fifteen years of marriage. My father and I came to blows on the patio of our double-wide trailer in south Tucson, creating a chasm between us. He left the three of us following that event. The physical confrontation between my father and me remain an ingrained memory packed with emotions that have been a source of regret and pain since the day it happened. In this physical conflict, I held a cinder block poised over his skull with threats to drive it through if he didn't leave, after physically subduing him to the ground.

As I've come to understand, this was one of the most traumatic, emotional nights of my life and has left a powerful emotional imprint that strongly influenced my relationship with my own sons decades later. My takeaway here was the influence of emotions on the physical body and mind. During the event, I remember being unable to think about anything other than his destruction.

At this point in my life, I began to quash the voices in my head with alcohol and tobacco, which ultimately led to high powered drugs, leading to my incarceration. During this period of hard drug usage, I found images and voices of ancestors I could not understand at the time. Fortunately, they remained in my mind until much later when they would all make sense. During my incarceration, looking back, my connection to the Landvætti had not been severed. They used their powers of suggestion to convince the district judge to offer me a way out by serving my country as a US Marine. The unfortunate effect of that decision was a tour spent addicted to high powered drugs, all to quash the voices in my head and quell the feeling of my heart constantly breaking, even though I had no idea why. While there were fleeting moments of clarity and understanding during my tour in the Corps, most of it was spent acquiring or recovering from the effects of cocaine and then heroin as I continued to attempt to silence the voices and feelings.

The intrinsic ability of an empath can lead to a sometimes violent attempt to break free of those feelings, particularly in younger minds who haven't grasped the gift of empathy. This leads to a polarization of life trajectories, as these individuals seek to either fully embrace or entirely reject the constant flood of emotional overload that can accompany this ability. In addition, without the proper education as to large groups, or the controls necessary for interacting with high-energy individuals, empaths can find themselves overwhelmed in much the same way we've heard about suffering from traumatic stress disorders.

> I was discharged with an "other than honorable conditions" for lack of self-control, as I was on a wide, self-destructive streak. I returned to Tucson forty days prior to my father succumbing to end stage renal failure; he left this plane without us finding peace. My young, impatient mind interpreted as being "inconvenienced" by providing for his daily needs, all the while understanding of his destruction pulling my heart apart. Without a close comparison, the most emotionally difficult forty days of my life.

My father and I were never close in those later years, as he chose to keep the display of emotions limited to anger and disgust. Many years later, when Óðinn made his presence to me, I learned that my father had rejected his cultural heritage that had been transferred through the generations from his grandmother. I now know his alcoholism was caused by his desire to quash the voices, followed by an extended period of regret, because as life would have it, I would follow in his footsteps.

> During my father's funeral, I was handed the folded flag (my father had served in the US Army). It was then my father came to me. I could see him as clear as the other physical entities who had been in the room earlier. His haggard looks, frail figure stood before me as I alone knelt before the stand with his urn placed atop of it. He gazed at me and smiled. I broke down into tears from both having the feelings I did about him and the fact that I could see him. I personally believe that this was one of those moments that created a crack in my armor of denial.
> Following my father's funeral and wake, I spent the next several years on a full-out self-destructive sequence, riding super-fast motorcycles and taking high powered narcotics covered in large quantities of alcohol. Weeklong benders had me waking up in strange places as I sought suicide by motorcycle. This lifestyle led to a heroin overdose in a south Tucson drain culvert in late September 1989.

But the Landvætti found me again, and with the power of Óðinn (my deity), I was delivered from that life. My self-destruct sequence enlightened me to my uniqueness, but more importantly in hindsight, I now see that I needed a hard break to this behavior and thought process to move past it.

> The deliverance came in the form of a grungy biker who found me, picked me up, dragged me to his mobile home in south Tucson, and locked me in a bedroom with a bathroom. For two months, I anguished for hours, slaying the demons of my mind that I had been avoiding, arriving at a place where I could see the spiritual realm again. Although I didn't understand the correlation to where I was, I did note it was a place without the emotional turmoil that I was living in. I enjoyed Thanksgiving 1989 with Grobber and his wonderful ole lady (Marie) for the first time in ten years, clean and sober. This had been my introduction to the

positivity of dark energy of the universe. The death of previous behaviors or mental states, allowing for a re-birth, or birth of new systems that were put in place.

The reason I tell this story is that I believe it teaches us many lessons we need to understand. The first of these lessons is that our spiritual entities will never forsake us, as they are here to help us navigate through the understanding of the emotional experiences, as we will need to have an empathetic heart and mind when we are done with this lifetime and join our ancestors. Another powerful lesson we can take away from this story is the basic principle that, as spiritual beings with the free will to change our trajectory, we always retain the power to turn life's negatives into a learning opportunity that will help us grow, even if those lessons are learned in hindsight. However, I think there are other lessons as well, lessons as to how to better utilize our spiritual interactivity. I believe that one of the important keys to understand is the acceptance that everything we've heard may, or may not, be true for our individual chemical composition. We each need to take an intrinsic inventory of our unique beliefs and not be swayed by what is happening around us at any one time.

There have been other opportunities since those early days that created additional emotional cornerstones in my mind. I've come to the interesting understanding that the spiritual entities around me, as well as physical entities, have been working in concert to keep my spiritual and empathetic education moving forward.

> I admit that next to my father's passing from this plane, the single largest emotional gift that I embraced was meeting and marrying my wonderful wife (of now over 32 years). During the early years of our marriage, we struggled as I intellectually matured; however, her spiritual aura taught me so much. I can hardly begin to express the impact she has had on my personal interpretation of all things. A devout Christian, her capacity for understanding and forgiveness is beyond human comprehension. Her spiritual core fostered my education in ways I've yet to fully

grasp, but her legitimacy has been confirmed by the Landvætti repeatedly throughout our lives together.

Herein lies another critical key to understanding spirituality. Accept others the way they are. As spiritual entities, our lessons in empathy do not include the need to save anyone, as we are all just here to understand emotion's effect on our knowledge. By utilizing the power of understanding and compassion, we accept the responsibility for allowing others to find their own way spiritually, providing them with examples as to what has successfully worked for us. Much the same way we would in an academic setting by assisting our classmates in understanding the lessons of that day. Because of our unique genetic chemistry, our interpretation of spiritual communications is fundamentally different than others. Most individuals who profess to be monotheists remain tangled within the religious practice and not the underlying theology.

Books about spirituality should strive to separate the theology or spiritual beliefs from the practice or public displays of a religion. To begin our discussion about spirituality in earnest, we must understand what theology means in the modern day. First, let's look at where some who struggle with theology are.

Seasonal Rhythm

Everything within the physical plane has a reason, and like those reasons, the rhythm of the universe and the earth's breathing can be felt through the seasons. Even in the consideration of night and day, we find a repeated rhythm. This is balance. The universe strives to remain in balance, and catastrophic events occur when it comes out of balance. This is a known fact of the universe, and of Mother Earth.

If we truly live intentionally, we must embrace this rhythm. We must understand it at its deepest center. The rhythm of the universe is omnipresent and unrelenting from our physical perspective. It just "is" from the other plane's perspectives.

Blame and Credit

This has become one of the mainstays within the modern religious practices and is fairly debated as to its validity. However, I believe it remains a strong influence on practitioner behavior worldwide. The idea of falling short of expectations was in place by parents long before monotheistic practices came along; however, it was perfected at a society level and implemented as methods of control by a limited few with the new religious practices. The idea that credit for life's successes could be passed up to a deity, while the blame of failure remains on the shoulders of the individual, creates an imbalance at its very core. Accepting blame, and therefore extrinsically assigned shame, for a perceived slight before one's physical existence is certainly a way to reduce the self-esteem of the general population and make it easier to establish mental control. This is another negative aspect of many practices who manipulate the truth for reasons other than true growth of the individuals.

This is where my beliefs stray from most mainstream ideas: i I don't accept shame for things I may have done that violates a rule I don't subscribe to, especially when I did it honorably, with my family in my heart, within the limits of societal laws. While I do encounter guilt (i.e., forgetting to put the toilet seat down, etc.), the idea is that after learning the necessary lesson from whatever task, I remove it from my conscious and unconscious mind, freeing my mind to process other incoming sensory input. The easiest way to understand the guilt/shame cycle is the bi-directional process involved in being influenced by shame to acquire a level of guilt.

Shame, as an idea of control, is an extrinsic control that attempts to force a behavior change in another. This is the societal control where others attempt to change our behavior or thought processes. Shame typically drives the other side of guilt.

Guilt is an intrinsic method of emotional teaching in our physical mind, attempting to alter our selves to behave or think a different way. Guilt is the control that many seek in their efforts at assigning shame. Guilt creates an emotional landmine within the human mind to alter our behavior.

Notice one is an extrinsic force, while the other is within ourselves? That's not an accident. That is how we have been programmed to function from a very young age. Our parental figures attempt to shame our behavior, hoping to instill a level of guilt that will alter our future behavior. If it is done with the individual in mind, it's positive, otherwise it's not.

Theology

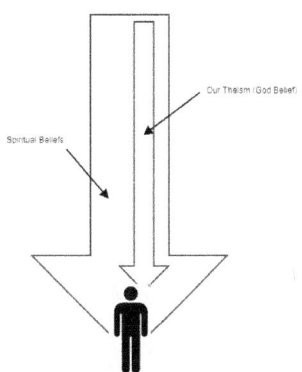

Figure 12 - *Understanding that our theism is a part of our overall spirituality is a critical key to success.*

The first point that we must all agree on is that there isn't a wrong theology or interpretation of a deity. Regardless of choosing to recognize none, one, or one hundred deities, that is your unique interpretation, and if those thoughts provide you with comfort and ease, then that is the theology for you. There is a difference between our theology and our spirituality, and it's completely acceptable to be different. Whereas our theology concentrates on the deity level of existence, our spiritual beliefs encompass both the deity and the spiritual planes of existence. Some may find themselves changing their theology throughout their physical lifetimes, vacillating between mono and polytheistic beliefs, maybe even dropping their belief in a deity all together. Arriving at the understanding as to what the theology is, we must look at a generic description as to what theology means. It may have a multitude of descriptions, and depending on who uses it within what context, the generic definition can barely scratch the surface.

Theology is defined as "the study of the nature of God and religious belief". As per Merriam Webster's dictionary, this is the publicly accepted definition of theology.

Modern-day theology has become more about the practice than the understandings. Identifying the difference between what we believe theology is about is a much larger intrinsic look at what we think we know. Because of its highly personal nature, many have chosen to forego that deeper discussion in lieu of following the other members. This is where we find most mainstream practitioners.

As mentioned earlier and certainly later, the theology within what we know as spirituality brings an understanding of a deity figure and the beliefs as to how that deity expects us (the practitioners) to behave toward them or as a representative of them. According to most theologians, there are three major branches of these theological beliefs:

1. Absence of Gods. Typically referred to as atheism by academia. There are also many practices who have subscribed to this form of underlying theology, including some forms who propose that the world is simply spiritual in nature and doesn't recognize a centralized deity figure(s).
2. Mono (or one). Monotheism is the primary understanding in modern culture, as the mainstream, organized religions all share this at their core. In addition, we find many other (including most indigenous beliefs) practices subscribing to this theology. Whereas the deity's name is irrelevant (for this discussion), the idea that there is a singular deity (or creator) is at the root of their beliefs is what defines it as monotheism.
3. Poly (or many). While many of the polytheistic beliefs and practices have faded into the annuls of antiquity, there remain some practices that still subscribe to this theology. Many have identified Hinduism as a possible contradiction to the tenements of the definition of poly, while others have claimed it to be. This will be discussed further when we discuss the ideas of our perspectives. The idea that as one gazes upon the deity

figure, one can ascertain different aspects and interpret them as different entities, makes absolute sense. In addition, we are currently witnessing a resurgence with the adoption of some of these practices, particularly with the polytheistic practices of ancient Greece and Scandinavia. One might say that I fall into this category as I recognize two deity figures personally as I seek to find balance in our existence.

As one can quickly ascertain, there is a substantial spectrum of beliefs surrounding the inclusion of a deity, or deities, or a lack thereof. How we translate our interaction with the deity level should be a very intimate thing and not predicated by our inclusion in some practice affiliation. We'll discuss the planes of existence later; however, our personal interpretation of our spiritual influences and/or our communications dictates which theology we subscribe to. More importantly, having the intrinsic understanding of separating our theology from those age-old practices is critical for each of us. Our theology should match our feelings as to how we believe. The heart, the mind, and the personal spirit should all agree on our beliefs, ensuring that we don't confuse the perceived necessity of the social inclusion with our intrinsic need for spiritual understanding. To fully understand the real definition of our beliefs, we must be reminded of the other side with the forced religious practices that came to power in the early days of the current geological epoch in an earlier discussion.

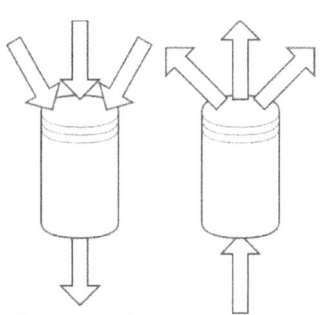

Figure 13 - *Our communications with our deities could be multiple entities sharing the channel.*

To fully grasp what we think we know about our spirituality, we must spend time exploring our theology. Understanding our intimate relationship with our deity is critical to recognizing our interpretation. When we consider our own theology, our understanding is formulated about how we interact with the world. From aura creation and projection to energizing spiritual entities around us to obtaining our core theology (what god or gods we believe in). To effectively do this, one must set aside the practices that have been handed down through millennia of generations and determine what part of spirituality we believe. While subscribing to the practice demonstrates our willingness to be a part of a social group, understanding the underlying beliefs is what separates the theology from the practice. This is where we can begin to gather our knowledge about what we believe. Exercises like meditation and prayer can help us obtain focus to determine what we feel is right about the many facets of spirituality. The good news here is that because it is a very personally intimate relationship, there is no wrong answer.

To fully understand the breadth of a deity from the millions of physical beings who have seen him/them is to gather hundreds of people around a canyon and have them gaze across it. Each retells their perspective of overlooking the canyon. They each see it differently. This is the same way we gaze upon our deity(s). We can choose to stay in our place and continue to see him/them the same way all the time, or we may change our perspective and see them differently. Ultimately, we are still gazing upon the face of infinity.

I believe that another piece of misinformation that has surfaced over the last couple of thousand years is that once you have declared your allegiance to a singular form of theism, whether it be mono, poly, or absentia, you are condemned to remain that for eternity. That is not how our existence works. As we move through our lives, our perspectives change, in much the same way it would look at anything else. As our perspective changes, so too might the relationship we have with our deity. That relationship retains the ability to change and evolve as we do. Because we have a relationship with an infinite being, our perspective of that deity may change, much the same way our perspective changes about our physical parents throughout our lifetimes.

Separating Theology From The Practice

Having discussed the negative connotations of religious practices that evolved alongside our spiritual understandings of our own theology, we need to look at separating our personal theology from religious practices.

Many religious bodies are typically more focused on the practice than they are with their personal interaction with this god(s), as some see them as being one and the same. In most cases, practitioners are taught the maintenance practices from previous generations. This is expected as part of the collective experience of that group and happens long before practitioners are instructed in the actual theology, if the theology is ever instructed at all. The unfortunate reality of a religious practice that has been implemented is to drive the "train to maintain" mentality that has prevailed throughout the church leadership since antiquity. Churches sometimes focus their teaching on correcting others in lieu of the self. Try as we might, we lack the ability to "save" anyone spiritually. This fundamental issue escapes the modern church leadership. The best we can hope for is to educate them, and if they choose to listen, they will experience enlightenment, otherwise they will experience their fate. Mainstream practices have become an "us versus them," identifying anyone outside of the practice as needing to be saved. This is not a theology, it is part of the religious practice.

As mentioned earlier, theology is technically defined as the theory of how a deity interfaces with physical beings. The fundamental failure with ALL theologies is that it is the finite interpretation of an infinite mind. Where does theology stop and the practice start? Theology and the supporting spiritual beliefs should be deeply private and individual by their very nature. When considering the influence that our genetic chemical composition has on our understanding of the world around us, there is no rationale to enforce my beliefs on anyone else. The uniqueness of our knowledge structure makes for a very different interpretation than anyone else; therefore, when any perceived rule dictates another's spiritual behavior, one must immediately question its legitimacy. While conversations are expected, the idea that anyone would segregate another because of this is ludicrous and most unfortunate.

The unfortunate reality is that many who have subscribed to monotheistic practices are trapped within the vicious cycle that those practices are designed to create, and we know that the fear of eternal damnation looms heavily. The architects of those practices ensured that they created a cycle of recruitment and maintenance. However, the tide is changing throughout the world, leading many to seek answers outside of mainstream religion.

To clearly define the difference between a theology and its associated practice, one simply needs to ask, "what is my responsibility toward others?" If the answer includes "fix" or "save" them, that is the practice. If the answer is something like "demonstrate, but don't expect," this is more of a theological statement. The idea should always be that you are responsible for you. You should be free to explore any part of your spirituality without guilt or shame.

Individual theism that has been embraced by a multitude of practices is that of a single creator, and while that idea is a recognizable interpretation of a deity's communications with those on the spiritual plane, it is only one of the many possibilities.

One of the primary reasons I put much of the information here is so we have a detailed understanding of the influence religious practices have had throughout the millennia and we take care not to repeat history. Many have come to me to say they are discouraged by these practices, and they are trying to convince others of their new discoveries. Essentially, this suggests that we are simply supplanting one practice for another, which we know is not how this works. We have spoken throughout this text about the rules within the practices throughout the world. Spirituality and the freedom to have an individual relationship with our deity should not need any rules. We should be able to sing and dance from our heart and not a prescribed methodology of doing anything in a specific manner. I believe that this is the same slippery slope that monotheistic practices found themselves on, which led us to where we are today. Therefore, I suggest we study our beliefs more diligently to ensure we don't repeat history.

Birth of the Deity

While most of the spiritual practices of the earth recognize a centralized form of universal energy or a deity level of entities. Most disagree with how this deity came to be, and even more simply overlook it. However, the idea of intelligent design isn't too far off the mark, as the existence at one point was a collection of miniscule energy particles, a simple collection of molecules of energy, which we know can even happen in the vacuum of nothing.

Ultimately, these energies coagulated and drew more power into a collective. As deity level entities are not bound by time, there is no way to know about how long this took in physical plane years. However, within this coagulation of energy, there formed a consciousness.

Neither the spiritual layer nor the deity layer is bound by the rules of time and space, and here on the physical plane is the only place those laws apply.

This consciousness considered the necessity of form in this void. Ultimately, a second consciousness formed in a process of replication, essentially bundling all the energy of the universe into two equal parts. In my beliefs, traits were assigned to these two entities, traits that we see replicated in all their creations with both masculine and feminine characteristics. These characteristics would be used in almost every creation in all of existence. In my belief, these two original deities assumed these traits, one feminine and one masculine. This established a balance.

The second consciousness was formed as an equal balance for the first. These two consciousnesses possessed all the power of the universe and would become the first two deities. Now, depending on your beliefs, it's completely acceptable to have as many deities as you feel are right. It really doesn't matter. The idea that this entity or entities communicates with and helps you is what is important. My belief is based on my understanding of a universal necessity to retain a balance in all aspects of existence. Therefore, I was taught that there are a minimum of two deity entities.

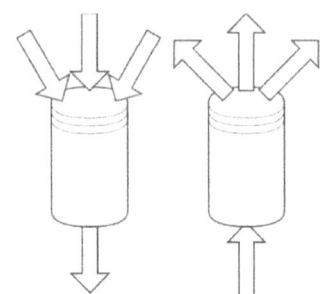

Figure 14 - *How the deity communications is understood is simply perspective.*

Why the confusion about single versus multiple deities? It's all in the perspective. In the case of a baseball team, when they are together, it is a singular entity: the team. When they are being addressed individually, we count the thirty or so people involved in the team as individuals. Same concept applies when dealing with deities. As shown in the image to the right, if one sees the communications from the bottom, it is understandable how the perception would be a singular entity, whereas if one was looking from the top, one understands the multiple communications happening. Individuals who don't feel that there are any centralized figures within their understanding are simply looking at what others may call animism by acknowledging all spiritual communications coming from spiritual entities and not a centralized one.

In my understanding, these two deities then dedicated some of each of their universal energy to create matter (the scientific definition). The matter they created was millions of times denser than anything we can conceive today and contained every unique molecule in all of existence. They then took their pieces of matter and smashed them together into what the scientific community calls the Big Bang theory and created our universe, or the physical plane. Within the construct of what was created, a framework of "time and space" was established for anything within this new universe. This also explains why the universe we know is still expanding, like ripples on a pond. The impact of the creation continues to expand outward.

Upon the creation of the universe, these deities then purposely cast energies into the spiritual plane, which then coagulated in much the same way the deities themselves had coagulated before, creating a collection of "entities" to help oversee this new universe. While these entities lacked the supreme power of the universe and had no form or bindings of the rules of this new universe, they shared in the infinite knowledge collective. The original two deities discovered procreation and created lifeforms similar in energy levels to themselves. These became the gods, or deity level entities (by legend). For those who celebrate the polytheistic beliefs, this is where all the gods descend from the first two. For those who believe in only one deity, my belief is that these entities created the additional spiritual sources identified above to obtain and maintain the knowledge of all that is, or ever will be.

The original deities then released additional energy sources again, and when they coagulated, the deities breathed a consciousness into them. Primitive at first, the deities created multiple physical life forms, infusing this life with the spiritual entities that they had created, to finally arrive at the "intelligent design" that would ultimately become the anatomical modern humans on earth. Throughout this time, they also created the building blocks that would become each type of plant, animal, and force within the universe. They instilled in each physical life form the power to procreate and a level of evolution and ensured that their ability to communicate with a bonded spiritual entity was embedded so it couldn't be removed.

They needed to keep things in place, so they dedicated spiritual entities to gravity, magnetism, as well as other natural forces within this new universe. They would go on to create, with the help of the spiritual realm that had become a by-product of their energy division. These original entities, either with or without the extreme power of the universe, had no concept of sensory input or emotion, but because of the knowledge and wisdom of everything that will ever be, they knew they needed a method of educating how to control emotions.

As the deities created physical life within the time and space boundaries, this ultimately formed the physical plane. The deities knew that the physical life forms would need guidance, in addition to the spiritual entities needing to be educated in the emotional differences among the physical plane, therefore they created a process to bind a spiritual entity with each physical lifeform's instinct for survival. In addition, the spiritual sources sought the sensory and chemical manipulations we call feelings, or the emotional response, as they had no experience in which to complete their understanding.

As we search for a way to understand the vastness of our definition of these deities, we have come to understand them as an infinite being. The full understanding of an infinite being, however, is a little more daunting to tackle.

Layers of Existence

In the beginning, during the creation of all of existence, the deity(s) created three layers of existence, which technically consisted of different universal energy levels. These three layers include:

1. Deity Layer where most of the entities are directly connected to the bulk of existence energy.

2. Spiritual Layer where the entities are a collection of miniscule levels of existence energy.

3. Physical Layer where the entities possess trace amounts of existence energy. However, because the physical entities were simply carrying vessels for spiritual entities,

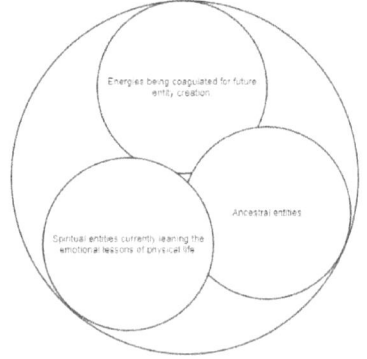

Figure 15 - *Understanding the multiple planes of existence is important to grasp.*

this plane and the spiritual realm overlapped closely.

The interactivity between layers of existence requires the universal energy to tap through. While the function of each layer serves a different need of existence, I am told that the Deities and the Landvætti ensure the appropriate amount of energy necessary at each level is associated with the right entities. In most cases, there are three forms of communications between these layers.

1. Deities communicate freely with the spiritual, and semi-frequently with the physical layers. This communication channel traverses both directions and allows the deities to hear the requests from other planes and speak to the other planes as well.
2. Spiritual entities communicate freely with either the deity or spiritual plane in a constant quest to understand how to operate on the physical plane.
3. Physical entities require their spiritual counterpart to communicate across to the other levels. This requirement technically means that physical entities do not broadcast a message but can receive communication from the other layers.

These layers of existence have very different but necessary functions within the scope of existence. The deity plane is reserved for the deities and the universal energies; outside of the deities, very few spirits have been elevated to this layer. The original spiritual entities created by the deities reside here, and although they do not wield the universal energy themselves, they do possess access to it. Deities wield all the energy of existence and grant additional energies to spiritual sources who are currently operating within the physical plane of existence.

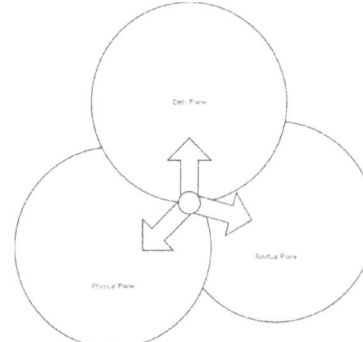

Figure 16 - *Understanding the spiritual realm is very important in plotting one's course of existence.*

Most of the existence is within the

spiritual realm (plane). Former physical existences, as well as future and present spiritual entities, reside in the spiritual realm. This realm is closely intertwined with the physical world, which fosters the potential for future conceptions, as well as those entities currently learning their emotional lessons of empathy. This indicates that we (as entities currently learning emotions) are closer to our ancestors than we know.

Communications between the layers of existence happen frequently and are typically broadcast across all three layers simultaneously. While the communications from the physical realm must travel through the spiritual plane to reach the deity layer, the connection between one's spiritual self should foster these communications.

Understanding the Aura

When our intrinsic spirit decides to reach out, it is more of a broadcast type of approach, where many different types of spiritual entities are available, in addition to the deities, for whatever type of request the physical entity has made through their spiritual self. There are also many occasions where two auras physically occupy the same space, and time and energy is transferred, consciously or not, between the physical entities.

The connection from one spiritual entity to another is caused by a polarity vacuum within the aura. An individual's aura consists of three (3) major factors:

1. Their spiritual belief,
2. Their emotional state,
3. Their spiritual experiences.

It can act as a repellant or vacuum to spiritual energies surrounding us. The aura could inquire of the other realms of existence by creating a vacuum of wisdom and knowledge, or it could seek physical manifestations or resource reallocations. The aura is an individual's spiritual environment and interactive interface to the other realms of existence (deity, spiritual) for a draw of knowledge. The connection between the aura of an individual and the spiritual realm occurs any time the aura on the physical plane creates a vacuum of wisdom or knowledge, whether the individual is aware of it or not. Whether there is belief in spirituality or not, this aura is constantly being projected into the other realms of existence.

Whenever an entity's aura creates a vacuum to the spiritual realm, it creates a vacuum to the deity realm as well. This connection to the deity realm may signal and receive the favor from that level whereby the deity will apply other realm's resources toward the or fulfillment. While rare, this situation does happen, particularly when individuals require some non-ordinary requirement.

The personal aura (Figure 17) demonstrates that it is a direct reflection of all our intrinsic energies projected into a spiritual bubble around us that represents who we are to the spiritual realm. Within the projected aura are a multitude of identifiers that alert the spiritual entities what and why we are making a particular request. However, what many may fail to understand is that the aura must replicate the need for the request, whatever it is. This is where many miscommunicate their request, and therefore do not feel that the request ever comes to fruition. The personal aura is the direct link between the spiritual entity currently residing the biological body and the other spiritual entities around us.

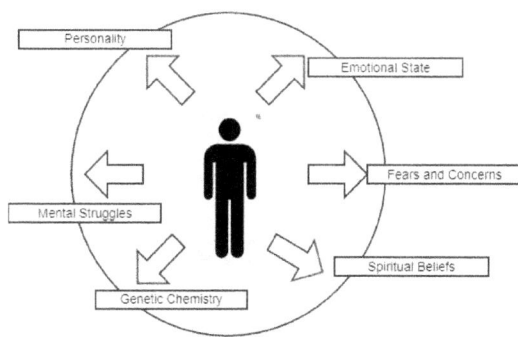

Figure 17 - *Demonstrates the Personal aura's display of intrinsic energies to the spiritual world.*

As for our personal aura, it is both an outbound and inbound channel of communication between the individual entity and the spiritual world around us. Therefore, as other spiritual entities attempt to communicate with us, they interact with our aura. When these interactions occur, the input received is then passed into the physical body's neural pathway identically to the way our physical sensory signaling occurs, thereby being interpreted by the brain as physical sensory input. To this, many report having feelings or maybe glimpses and sounds that only affect them. This is because the aura passes the input into the neural pathway in such a way as to not be able to separate it from the physical sensory input. We'll discuss more about the physiological function of neural interpretations in a later chapter.

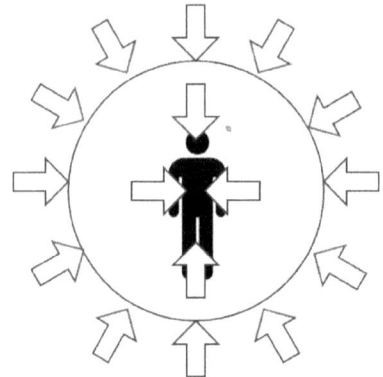

Figure 18 - *Spirits interact with our aura which is then interpreted by our physical sensory input.*

The aura is a central component for our physical body to interact with the spiritual or deity realms. Like other physical manifestations, the aura requires practice to perfect. In addition to the factors listed before, the management of the aura is controlled by managing the supporting components:

1. Fears and Concerns
2. Mental struggles
3. Personality
4. Genetic chemical interaction

We can only do a limited number of modifications for our genetics, but by altering our emotional state, we release a chemical maelstrom into the bloodstream, knowing that increased exposure to the chemical mix may ultimately alter our genetic code, thereby altering what we project in our personal aura. While I discourage the use of drugs and/or alcohol when focusing on one's aura, many of the Landvætti that I have come to know and work with are fine with me having a few drinks while we're talking. Many within the spiritualist's practice discourage, and I agree, the use of illegal drugs. You are capable of making your own choices, hopefully remembering that there may be ramifications for those choices. The other side of this is knowing that should you decide that you require the alteration of the mind to focus on your aura, then the chance is very high that you haven't cleared item #2 from the list above. Again, you need to be sure you are producing the right message to the spiritual world through your aura if you are expecting anything positive in return. However, our aura broadcasts at a particular frequency based on how we are projecting it. Understanding how frequency matching fosters communications with certain entities will make it easier to understand why we seem to connect to some but not others.

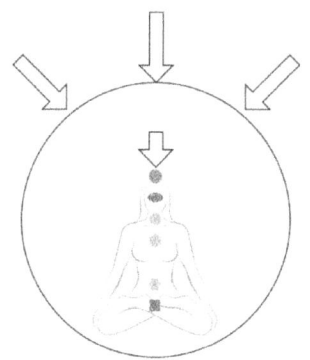

Figure 19 - *The Aura passes energy received through to the Chakras (or gates) in the body.*

The aura relies on the spiritual self based on the physical mind to project either a transparent aura that clear communications can pass through or a cloudy aura that hampers communications and can cause issues like we learned about emotions. Clarity of one's aura is established by the clarity within the physical mind of the individual. If the individual can control the emotional storms and obtain a peaceful environment within the mind, the aura becomes transparent and spiritual communications are clearly understood. This level of clarity within the mind and aura produces a frequency of broadcast that becomes more aligned with the frequency of Mother Earth.

The aura is the connection between the energy of the spiritual realm and the individual self. The individual self contains several "gates" for spiritual energy passing through it. This is the study of the chakras. There are seven chakras, and some contend that the aura itself is one of the chakras, making that eight. I agree. The aura is an invisible, spiritual globe that surrounds the spiritual entity that then provides an interface to pass the universal life energy through to the crown chakra, or top of our head. The chakras should be in a constant state of free movement, allowing the energy to pass freely from one to the next, ultimately passing the healing energy from the universe to all the chakras from the crown all the way to the root or sacral.

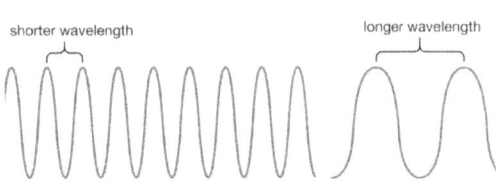

Figure 20 - *Because the auras broadcast on a particular frequency, we may find "love at first sight".*

Frequency Matching

Our aura is projected into the spiritual realm using a certain wavelength or frequency. It's the exact same theory for broadcasting any other message. For those of you who may be unfamiliar with wavelengths, energy is transmitted through the air at certain frequencies, meaning that there is a defined height and length of the signal wave. The frequency at which our aura is projected is dependent on our emotional state at the time and may fluctuate throughout the day, as our emotional states adjust to the challenges we face. These frequencies changes are very important, as they determine other spiritual interactions with those around us.

When our aura locates other entities or other ripples that match its frequency, we have joy, or depending how close the individual frequency matches ours, we may have a higher level of likeability. Therefore, we may find particular songs just strike us and others don't. This also explains why within a room full of people, we will feel drawn to a handful, while the remainder we do not, and certain people within the room may repel us. All of this is dictated by the interpretations of our frequency matching and is part of the aura projection.

Social interaction through one's aura creates a secondary level of understanding others. While the spiritual entities provide us with the understanding of their aura, it supports or conflicts with our physical sensory input as it's stored in the brain. This is the explanation of how some may feel about a used-car salesman. No offense to individuals of that profession. When the surface (physical sensory input of vision) provides an understanding of a reputable individual, the aura may absorb the understanding that the individual simply views us as another sucker to help make a sales quota. The aura presents itself physically sometimes as well, by creating involuntary micro expressions of the physical self that others are trained in, that can reveal our motives when interacting with them.

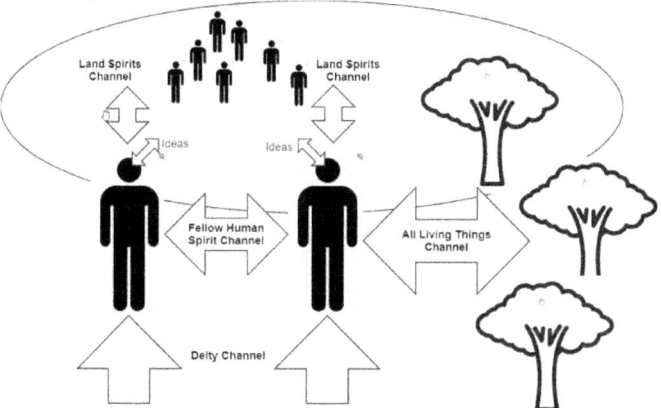

Figure 21 - *Spiritual influences are all around us on the physical plane. Understanding them is a critical key to happiness.*

Spiritual Beliefs

When attempting to understand our own spiritual beliefs, one needs to strip away the practice part of religion to discover what we actually know about the underlying theology. Once we understand the connection between the deity layer and us, true enlightenment can occur.

A spiritual entity's purpose in interfacing with the physical plane is to fulfill a void created by either a physical entity's material request or intellectual knowledge requests created. There are several layers of interaction that the spiritual entities have with us that can potentially modify our emotional states, thereby altering the sensory input stored within our brain as memory bits. So, we create the vacuum necessary to draw in the spiritual entity that explains why and when we need to do this, as well as the benefit to our emotional connectivity.

Armed with an understanding of the brutal enforcement of these new practices from the previous chapter, let us step sideways to speak about the definition of the theology or spirits. According to beliefs throughout the history of the world, we find an understanding of spirituality came to those early humans, particularly as they transitioned from hunter/gatherers to the agriculture/herder lifestyles about 11,000 years ago. While there is very little written record at that time, there is a substantial number of later writings that demonstrate the evolution of spiritual theory and understanding that we can extrapolate where these theories were derived from, as well as to the content of the original principles.

Spirituality is the belief and understanding in a spiritual world, whether as a separate plane of existence or as a separate group on the physical plane. In some understandings, we find that certain beliefs focus on just spiritual entities and their connections to the physical world. However, as it has been revealed to me, as a physical container bound to a spiritual entity, we gain knowledge about ourselves. Within the understanding of spirituality, we find nestled in the pages an idea of a deity and therefore a theology of our own. While the study of a deity is in another section here, the many entities that exist between the deity and us are open to discussion. Whether you call them angels or spirits, the concept is essentially is the same. They are entities that are neither a human nor a deity.

There any several types of entities we should recognize from the spiritual plane.

1. Land Spirits, or as I've come to know them, the Landvætti. These spiritual entities were created the same way all others are created (including the process that created the original deities described in detail in an earlier section) and are given all the

wisdom and knowledge of what will be from the deities who created them. Their overall function when visiting the physical plane is to provide wisdom and knowledge to whoever seeks it. These spiritual entities are not experienced with emotional intellect at all, as they have never experienced physical life, but have pure knowledge and wisdom without the interference of emotional alterations.

2. Every other form of life, past, present, and future. All other entities of life experience the same creation process and their own method of emotional empathy. Each blade of grass. Each tree upon the land. Every life on the physical plane of existence possesses an aura that can communicate with the spiritual realm, as well as with others here on the physical plane. The ancestors and other life form entities possess emotional intelligence because of their experiences on the physical plane and want to share it with physical entities. Most of these entities possess the empathy necessary to receive communications from those on the physical plane.

3. Deity or deities, as we are all familiar with these. Whether you interpret the influence you receive as a singular entity or multiple entities is irrelevant in this conversation; knowing that the deity level is different than the other levels is what is important.

Within the idea of spirituality lies the hopes for eternal life, as well as peace and comfort from both rational and irrational fears during this physical lifetime and beyond. Some have prayed to their idea of a deity in hopes of obtaining wealth or fame or material gains, as well as emotional balance. This underscores the necessity of believing in an idea larger and stronger than oneself. When fully considering the idea behind spirituality, one needs to fully understand where this belief comes from. We discussed the evolution of psychology, both from the human and animal kingdom perspectives, as well as other understandings given to me by the Landvætti.

Biological bodies live on the physical plane of existence, and they are bound by the rules of time and space. They gain knowledge and wisdom by sensory interactions with the physical world around them and develop the chemical manipulations necessary to create emotions based on these sensory inputs, which are a prized possession of some spirits and are referred to as life's experiences. These experiences are interlaced with the genetic chemical composition of the biological body, which alters the sensory input prior to its storage as knowledge, which means that no one contains the exact same data.

Most humans are oblivious to any other life form's spirituality, physical or on other planes of existence. While many report that they have "better feelings" with pets or plants or being in the outdoors, they fail to recognize the spirits within those entities are producing an aura of peace and harmony. Throughout the evolution of humans, they have become increasingly arrogant, surrendering the instinctual thought process and replacing it with an initially strong spiritual connection, which has degraded throughout the millennia. They have opted to disregard the natural world and instead attempt to conquer it.

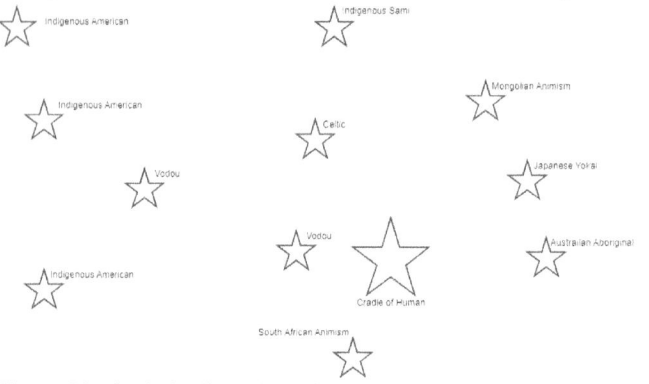

Figure 22 - *Societies throughout the world seem to have a very similar view of spirituality when separating it from the practices.*

The early explorers left familiar grounds and people to set out and discover additional locations for hunting and resources. These early humans ultimately settled in the four corners of the earth, far from anyone or anything familiar, and in most cases, far from anything at all. In addition, as these early settlers created their new lives throughout the world, a common language had yet to develop. While the historical record shows many drawings appearing throughout the world, even further back than our explorers, the consistent possibility of transferring ideas and concepts, particularly of a detailed spiritual nature, would have been very limited. This leads us to believe that these early explorers might have experienced real-world interaction with spiritual entities who provided them with the knowledge to evolve further.

Herein lies the strongest evidence to date about the influence the spiritual realm has had on the physical one. Almost all (99.9%) of all these different early societies seem to come to an independent agreement about the spiritual interactivity. Why? It is my understanding that the channel from one's aura to the spiritual world was further revealed as the instinctual thought process was peeled back during the evolution of cognitive thought. Therefore, as those earlier evolved hominids left Africa, they slowly diminished their natural instincts, which revealed a solid spiritual connection. Following this a little more, we can understand the spiritual connection shows that the aura is a channel that many spiritualists have identified where the physical entity reaches out to the spiritual realm. During the early evolution of the human brain, we see the split between the spiritual and the instinctual thought processes.

As we cast our glance across the broad spectrum of spiritual beliefs throughout the world, we drill down past the public display of the practices used to the theology or beliefs at the depth of their understanding. It is here that we begin to find many commonalities amongst all these beliefs, which then causes one to ponder, how? Is it because one person met with that group and took the ideas? Maybe. But this discussion point only works long after the indigenous beliefs began their practices in the four corners of the world. This idea doesn't account for these earlier beliefs, where not only did we have a substantial geographic separation, but we would have had a language barrier as well. This then comes down to one of a very few possibilities.

1. Individual groups developed a cognitive and spiritual thought

process at approximately the same time. Sure, that's possible, although highly unlikely. While they each would have experienced the natural world at the same rate of exposure, their predators would have been different, as well as the weather and many other factors minimizing that they adapted and learned at the same rate in these different societies.

2. As the tribes moved along their migratory paths, they kept the same belief system, whereas all the stalls (where groups would stop for long periods of time during their migration) and splinters (groups who separated from the main migratory groups) modified the practices while maintaining the base tenements. It's plausible, and if we were discussing three or four groups, yea maybe. But we are talking about over a dozen societies who all seem to have the same core beliefs.

3. Finally, could our ancestors have interacted with the spiritual entities themselves? To me, this seems much more plausible. Separated by thousands of miles, with limited means to convey ideas, with varied diets leading to different chemical compositions, leading to different thought processes, I am convinced that our ancestors throughout the world would have interacted with the spiritual entities in-person for assistance along their journeys.

Within the individual beliefs emerges a belief in a deity level entity. We don't know whether the discussion included the identification of one centralized deity entity, many, or no deities at all and only beliefs in the equal spirits throughout this plane of existence. This is where we begin to find the sacred commonality, where spirituality begins to unify individuals under the banner of our spiritual cohesion.

Let's talk about our individual process of spirituality and what we believe. While this topic may seem somewhat central to this section of the book, we need to be careful that we identify our understandings as to exactly what part of what we believe is our spirituality. While this may seem simplistic, the idea here is that those of us who were born and raised in first-world nations are typically instructed in our practices of religion from a very young age, even before we are even born into the world. Let's talk about what we truly believe. Many of us have been instructed from a very young age in the "practices" of our parent's religion, whether we choose to be a part of the religious practice or not, the assigned value statements were embedded within our psyche.

Our theology is how we intrinsically believe our deity communicates with us. It centers around the idea of the type of information we receive in these communications, and then what we do with the information when we receive it. To get a better understanding, we need to consider the individual aura, our spiritual sense, providing the connectivity between the other planes of existence, as well as some interactivity on the physical plane. As mentioned earlier in the section about our aura, it is primarily constructed using our current mental state and spiritual beliefs, therefore how we interact with the spiritual world is completely hinged on our projection of the right type of energy.

Spiritual Energy

As mentioned in the previous sections, our deities were originally a collection of energy particles that coagulated to form a consciousness and became self-aware. In the same way, our spiritual self was formed. What this means is that a similar source of energy used by the deities to coagulate remains unassociated with a singular object or entity. This is the energy that is collected by the self or by another spiritual entity when it is needed. We've already discussed the aura and its function when passing this energy through to the Chakras, which is what generates the healing energy needed for spiritual healing practices.

In all instances, the spiritual entities within each of the groups identified earlier have both a lighter (positive) and an opposite darker (negative) energy associated with them. These darker energies do not always have the best interest of those physical entities who summon them, even by accident. However, while negative or dark energies may produce a concept of, there is no "evil" energy. More about this in a moment; suffice to say, there isn't any evil energy in the universe. The intent of the requestor is what defines the energy as "good or bad".

While energy can have light and dark properties, dark energy is not evil or even bad. Death must precede birth, and one must destroy one state to enter another. While we all seek to find lighter energy, there must be a dark side to provide the polarity. When we cast spells or utter prayers, we must destroy a previous state to enter the new one. The dark energy prevents the previous state from being perpetual and encourages new creation. It is this matter of fact with spiritual energy that we must understand if we seek to bring new things into our lives.

Within the idea of energy management, we need to understand that each of us possesses several portions of energy at some point, and each is critical to manage:

1. Parental portions. Each of our biological parent's supply fragments of their universal energy, which is involved in the conception of the biological unit.
2. Deity portions. Each of us possesses a portion of universal energy given to our spiritual entity prior to binding to the biological body, after biological conception occurs.
3. Spiritual portions. As a coagulation of transient energy bits then form our consciousness, our spiritual entity maintains these portions of energy throughout our existence. In addition, other spiritual sources may provide us with spiritual energy in a method described later called "assistive energy."

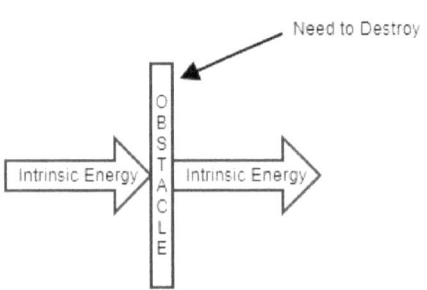

Figure 23 – *Inadvertently, some will place obstacles in place of the energy path.*

Our intrinsic energy is used in a multitude of ways. A portion of it is used for creating request vacuums from the spiritual realm, and more is used for casting spells and answering prayers. All these requests task the intrinsic spiritual energy, but other entities around us pass on their request energies from time to time that recharge our energy sources, as well as certain emotional values may recharge our intrinsic energies as well.

While we may now know how we get our energy, managing it is another matter that needs contemplation. Because many have an unfamiliarity with their intrinsic energy management, they may adversely place obstacles in the path of sending their energy to support their prayers or spells. What this means in the inner workings of prayers and spells is that, although we pray for something like "lots of money," we tell ourselves that we are "not worth it." This thought process then creates an obstacle. This obstacle needs to be destroyed for us to enjoy the successful obtainment of our prayer. The darker energy mentioned before comes in handy for this type of thing. By creating enough intent (want), our aura can use the dark energy to reduce the obstacle enough to allow the transference of energy to the aura, then out to the prayer support and ultimately fruition.

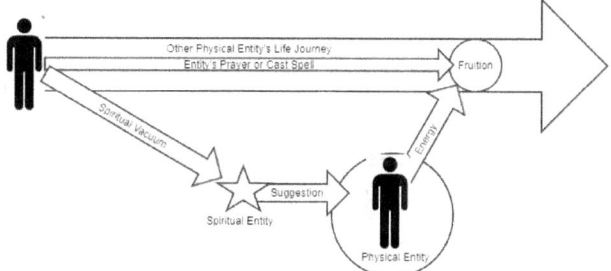

Figure 24 - *Assistive energy may be provided by others on the path to prayer/spell completion.*

Another example would be when we ask to "know something." When we simply ponder what it would be, the energy assigned to the task is very nominal, informing the spiritual realm that we are not interested. Whereas when we apply intent, additional energy is applied to the request, creating a more powerful vacuum, attracting more Landvætti to assist with the request.

Spiritual energy may also be provided and/or received by other physical entities in the path of a prayer or spell manifestation. Consider the example of needing a horse for a long journey. If you utter a prayer or cast a spell, the spiritual entities will begin to connect with physical or spiritual entities along the path who are open to suggestion, allowing for the resources to be made available for the individual who requested it. In addition, these individuals may provide some of their own energy, reducing the necessity to the issuer. This is called "assistive energy" and if one contemplates the number of individuals between the issuer and the completion, the potential additional energy from them may be substantial by the time we get to the actual manifestation.

At this point, let's see a more in-depth explanation of the polarity of the energy received.

- Light (Positive). This type of energy surrounds us. It is provided by all the spiritual sources throughout all of existence. Light energy is rejuvenation, healing, and growth. Light is given to the day to allow all life to flourish on the physical plane. Most energy transferred between entities of different planes contains positive energy. Also contained within the energy of light is joy, peace, and happiness, but a balance is always required, for we cannot have light without dark.
- Dark (Negative). This type of energy surrounds us on the physical plane, as it too is a natural part of the existence of all things. Dark energy is the transitions, death, decay, and the promotion of evolution, as it destroys previous states, allowing us to evolve and grow. Like the butterfly, we must first morph the caterpillar to be reborn into the beautiful butterfly. Dark energy also brings sadness and despair and can damage our hope. Therefore, it must be contained within our spiritual channels.

Spiritual Connections

In almost every minute of every day, different spiritual entities are bidding for our attention. They address each of us from a multitude of perspectives. Sometimes they are answering our requests, and sometimes they are answering other people's requests, using us as a resource to physically complete the request. In most cases, the spirits that interact with us the most are either:

- Other entities on the physical plane using the interfacing of personal auras to get and receive information;

- Entities who have moved beyond their physical lives to the spiritual realm and are deploying the power of suggestion from their empathetic understandings to either help us find the answer we seek or the results for someone else.

The Landvætti rarely fully interact with most of us after childhood, limiting themselves to a select few. Even more rare are a deity's direct interaction with those on the physical plane. I will tell you that it does indeed happen, it's just very rare. However, in some cases we find the ancestry spiritual entities reach out to the Landvætti for information necessary to fulfill a need on the physical plane.

Often people think that our communications with the spiritual world must be done with some type of ritual or prayer. This is one interpretation. Simply by having a thought, we can create a vacuum of knowledge that then signals the spiritual realm there is a need to be fulfilled. Sometimes, these requests can be perceived by other spiritual sources here with us. Whether these other sources are human or not becomes irrelevant. What matters is the fact that our thoughts and desires are broadcast for others to perceive. While many are too focused on personal material gains, there are those who can perceive these thoughts and/or concepts. These are very basic communications in the spiritual realm, and any who know how to listen may do so.

The overall purpose of our spiritual connections is to encourage the betterment of humankind via their inter connectivity with all the spiritual beings on earth. When considering the spiritual connectivity necessary both on the physical and spiritual plane, we need to consider how we power our connectivity and the energy necessary for managing our spiritual associations.

Also, when additional entities similar requests (planned or not) are incanted, this magnification of energy sources is then bound to the task, reducing the individual needs. This was the underlying concept with Galðr magic, or worship. By adding more voices to the prayers and/or spells, the increased energy multiplied its potential for successful completion.

The Puddle

Many amongst us have determined that their perspective of spirituality is the only one, or the most correct method of recognizing the deity(s). They have placed mental blinders on themselves to ensure that they do not alter their perspective for one reason or another. In many cases, they have been taught since before they were born that other perspectives were bad or evil.

This brings to my mind the story of "the puddle". This is more of a parable for us to learn from.

Imagine nine people standing in a circle around a puddle of rainwater. Each person gazes into the puddle. They learn everything there is to see from their unique perspective of the body of water. One sees the reflection of the sky and clouds on the surface of the water. They may see the reflection of the person standing across the puddle from them.

If, during this gaze into the puddle, we decide to exercise our free will, and step to the left one position, our perspective changes. We may see a different individual on the surface of the water, as well as a different view of the clouds. This has now expanded our perspective of the puddle. While we have increased our understanding, the puddle remains the same. As we continue to move around the circle of individuals, our understanding of the puddle continues to grow. The puddle remains the same, but our understanding of the breadth of the puddle evolves. When we arrive back at our original position, after circling the puddle, we have achieved a full understanding of the puddle.

This story speaks to us about the benefit of seeing our spirituality from different perspectives, which then gives us a greater understanding of our beliefs. But there is another perspective in this situation.

Upon returning to our original position in relation to the puddle, what if we turn to our right and ask the person next to us what they saw in the puddle? Knowing what we learned in the previous chapters, we know that our emotional state of control alters our physical sensory input, altering what we see and understand. This opening of one's heart to accept another's perspective of the puddle provides additional understandings as to the value of the puddle. As we continue to inquire of others, we broaden our understanding. This expanded understanding allows us to assist others in recognizing other perspectives without any form of judgment.

The puddle represents our beliefs. As an example, if we were to replace the puddle with our idea of a deity, by seeing that deity from different perspectives, we gain a more in-depth understanding of the deity figure. However, the key to the puddle is understanding that there are different perspectives to everything. We should all seek to embrace different perspectives as much as possible. Note: the idea of seeing our deity from a different perspective doesn't make our original perspective wrong, nor does it mean that these other perspectives are wrong either, just different. Instead of looking for differences, one needs to seek commonality.

Summary

How we see our deity is not nearly as important as what we do with the knowledge and wisdom they offer us. Having an in-depth understanding of how spirituality interacts with us daily helps us to better control our emotional state, which is then projected to the spiritual realm via our personal aura. By having a better understanding as to how our personal aura works, we can have more clear, concise knowledge transfers between our spiritual entities and ourselves, thereby helping us to live in harmony and intrinsic peace. Hopefully, the information contained within this section helps us to understand that our spiritual differences are not that different, after we get past the control methods of monotheistic practices that have been implemented in conjunction with many theologies over the millennia. As formless spiritual beings, we have no need for discrimination because of any physical characteristic and should seek to unify all peoples in a peaceful existence of learning and growth.

Our ability to find a peaceful co-existence starts with being peaceful within our minds. By understanding emotional control from the previous chapter, we can learn to listen with our heart for the advice from our ancestors, as well as other spiritual entities who offer ways to find harmony within our communities, with others searching for the same thing.

Our understanding and engagement in our personal spirituality is an intimately personal journey that should bring us inner peace and tranquility, as well as an abundance of knowledge and wisdom. The interpretation we receive from our spirituality helps us to understand our role as emotional students who exist on this plane of existence to learn empathy, so we may benefit others in the pursuit of their dreams and understandings.

EXERCISES

Chapter 4: Seeking Answers from the previous chapter

The information that you obtained should begin to connect you to the real crux of this book, and that is a view of your spirituality, which some may have said they didn't have. There are no right or wrong answers, only an alignment with the cornerstones of your belief system. It really doesn't matter who you refer to as your god, it only matters about the inclusivity that the message shares. The idea of using empathy to connect with others means that we also take their emotional status into consideration when interacting with them. This is the other part of empathy: learning to listen with one's heart instead of ears. The exercise of reaching out across the spiritual realm to communicate will work substantially better when the person is someone you care about; however, there may be individuals whom we discover that we didn't know before, and that is a part of the spiritual journey.

The idea of being spiritual includes both the external forces (i.e., spiritual entities on and outside the physical plane), as well as the intrinsic energies of the spiritual self to communicate and work with the environment. Using empathy is when we employ the spiritual self to reach across that realm to communicate. This is really the definition of empathy.

Absorbing the Energy of this Knowledge

In this chapter, I have brought up the topic of religion as an organized practice and discussed the benefits of spirituality, not as a replacement for religion but for a deeper understanding of whatever religion meets your belief system criteria. Remember, belief has two cornerstones: makes sense in the mind and feels right in the heart. Many sing the praises for beliefs that they don't subscribe to, masking their thoughts with rote exercises taught by generations before them. Our questions here are going to be based a little deeper on our spiritual understandings:

1. Why do I believe in a god? How do I know he/she/they are real?

2. Do I feel fulfilled within my belief system as to what I understand? How?
3. Do I believe every part of the religious teachings? Why?
4. Do I recognize the difference between practice and spirituality in myself? How?
5. What do I believe about "after death"? Why?
6. What do I believe about "before birth"? Why?

This list of questions should lead you to a series of other questions, particularly in the main part of whatever doctrine you subscribe to. There are no right or wrong answers within this, as the recognition of a deity and their influence on our lives are universal to some degree. As you complete the exercise of questioning your beliefs in spirituality, you may experience uncomfortable feelings of uncertainty. This is completely normal.

Many people have confided in me that they are afraid to challenge their faith for fear of going to Hel. According to the legends of the Norse, Hel wasn't a bad place to be. It was warm, with plenty of food and fun. It was on the other side of Hel that things got a little dicey. Again, in the same way you've hopefully done in the previous chapters, note your answers to these questions and see if there are others that get down to your core. Believing something because someone else said it was right is an answer. Recognize what is within the comfort of your heart and mind.

Adopting the Successful Wisdom Using Meditation

Meditate on your questions and take time to deeply consider each one. We can now use our meditation to reach across the spiritual realm and speak directly with those who know first-hand the answers to the last two questions. Again, remove the physical sensory input from our minds. Find some noise canceling headsets and try to eliminate as much input as possible.

Close your eyes and focus on each question until something feels right. Focus on that item. Note everything you can about the answer. Remember the story of "The Puddle." We want to look at each idea and vision from every perspective. Feel it, first with your mind, then with your heart.

Chapter Five

Prayer, Worship & Magic

W*ithout a close comparison, this* is the part of my teachings that seems to draw the harshest criticism and rebuke from mainstream religious practice partitioners. I believe that these are simply misunderstandings that stem from the history of the blind following of some practices. Not all followers of modern-day practices are blind followers, but there have been generations who have forgotten the theological part, yet passed down the practices to be followed, sometimes by force. However, if one takes a moment to root through the historical records on such matters, one can quickly determine where the newer practices simply absorbed the practices of antiquity and rebranded them to fit into their narrative.

To fully understand the evolution of the practice of magic through the pre-Christian Europeans, we need to go back in time before the arrival of this new practice in northern Europe. Back to the days before the western Roman Empire influence spread throughout western Europe and ultimately failed in the southern and western parts of Europe. The Celtic-Germanic tribes inhabited the areas from what is today France and southern Germany (referred to in those days as Gaul). The lands were inhabited by Celtic and Aquitani tribes, encompassing present-day France, Belgium, Luxembourg, most of Switzerland, parts of Northern Italy and Germany west of the Rhine, all the way north to the British Isles. While the Romans and Germanic tribes committed many lives to the establishment of the borders of the western and northern expansion of Roman rule, we find significant early writings from Roman scribes that included the fear of the "Celtic Druids", who could have been easily compared to the shamans and medicine men of indigenous societies of the period. These entities operated throughout most of Europe, providing the population of the time with the necessary magical skills that were frequently practiced, as well as a spiritual understanding.

My ancestors used the Celtic magic of that day and time, and by its very definition fell into three (3) unique categories.

1. Seiðr magic was used for casting spells and relied on druid/magician's ability in reaching out to extrinsic spiritual entities for their energy. Essentially, this type of magic collaborated with the spiritual entities around them to bring the request to completion. This simply came down to reallocating resources already among the physical plane, not creating something new but simply encouraging the arrival into the magician's (or requestor's) path.
2. Spácraft magic was used for casting spells that utilized the druid/magician's intrinsic energies to bring the spell to fruition. This form's magician generated a focused stream of energy that manifested something from another location. We know that "creating something from nothing" required the intervention and provision by a deity level entity; however, the reallocation of resources already in existence could be managed by spiritual energies.
3. Galðr magic utilized song and larger numbers of magicians to provide supporting energy by multiplying exponentially the

energy applied to an incantation or prayer. By far the easiest form of magical energy generation was Galdr magic, as many danced and sang with music in celebrations. This was a form of Galdr magic frequently used in a multitude of directed rituals.

When discussing magic, we must understand magic. Let's call it what it is and take a moment to call out the modern manipulations of these earlier forms of magic to meet the narrative needed by these modern practices.

The Center of Beliefs: Mother Earth

Regardless of whether we are discussing the indigenous beliefs that initiated in northwestern Africa with the beginning of the migration of Anatomical Modern Humans or the multitudes of belief systems in all four corners of the world, ultimately, they all settle on the central understanding of the power of the earth. Both with the magic of my Celtic ancestry and the powers recognized by most indigenous understandings, we find the centralized figure of Mother Earth. Many beliefs focus on the spiritual energy that radiates from and encircles the earth we walk upon. This part of our beliefs is very important to understand whenever a discussion of magic arises. We should take time to recognize the energy that Mother Earth provides to each of us, as well as consider the care we take of our mother. As I've experienced more of my physical lifetime, I've come to recognize the value that my physical mother provides to me, the unconditional love she offers. This is the same mentality I have regarding my Mother Earth. As I consider the powers of magic and spiritual influences within my life, I am constantly reminded of the interactions I have with Mother Earth.

> *"We are born with two mothers. One of flesh whom provides for our physical life, the other of spirit who provides for our spiritual life. Both are critical to our survival, as we are brought from the breasts of Mother Earth, so shall we return to her upon the successful completion of our lessons here."*
>
> -Alaska Úlfhednar

Before diving too deeply into the underlying philosophy behind prayers, worship, and magic, I'd like to make sure we understand that although my ancestors and I believed in and used the many forms of magic, it was clearly understood how the spiritual entities were arranged in relationship to the magician. Many societies, both before and after, have had a similar relationship with the spiritual entities around them. These societies, like the indigenous peoples throughout the world, have a similar belief in the necessity of including the spirits of both ancestry and energy into their daily life. They counted on mother earth to provide for them, and brother sun. (The Golden World) or "sister moon" (The Silver World) all played roles in the people's everyday lives. In addition, many of these societies recognized the connection of auras (although they may have described it differently) to the animal kingdom for the animal's (potential) sacrifice to feed the peoples. To those individuals, this practice and understanding was their implementation of many of my beliefs. Again, while I may call it other things, the base premise was the same. Even though my beliefs came from the other side of mother earth and from the tongue of another language, it is in perfect parallel with what I know to be the universal truth of our existence here.

Prayer

Prayer is the modern, culturally sensitive translation of what Seiðr magic was in the days of my ancestors. My ancestors would have been knowledgeable and included the spiritual entities around them instead of relying on a designated deity on the receiving end. The premise of prayers is to incant (speak) a series of words to hopefully invoke the deity to perform some requested tasks, whatever that might be. The practice of prayer comes from these earlier Seiðr magic rituals of pre-Christian Europe. Seiðr magic (and identically prayers) utilizes extrinsic energy sources for the completion of a particular request, creating a vacuum through the personal aura. In other words, the issuer of a spell/prayer sends out the request to the universe and the spiritual entities around them then sees the request to completion, based on other factors. It is critical for the intent of the issuer to remain constantly engaged, thereby feeding their intrinsic universal energy to the completion of the prayer/spell. The additional aspect of this definition is to understand the use and application of *intent*. This is a purposeful communication with our deities and spiritual entities. By designating the prayer or spell, we signify our intent, which then applies a level of our universal energies in the application of the request.

Because the spiritual realm is closely related to both the spiritual and physical planes, the sharing of resources, and/or calling spiritual entities to provide for others, generates an additional boost of energy, allowing additional spiritual entities to be drawn into the vacuum created, enhancing the potential for completion. This is very important to understand about magic and/or prayers: we are fundamentally destined to help others, so by incanting spells or prayers for others, we increase the likeliness of success. This also brings a higher probability of a deity level entity to provide favor and therefore additional energies to the task of completing the request.

We must also consider establishing and maintaining the balance within the cosmos. When we consider the act of requesting energy from the universe, or the earth herself, we have typically heard about offering something in return. This is good stewardship, as we replace what others drain from the universe. However, in the use of magical spells, or prayers, we must remember that the universe, as well as the earth, offer energy for us every minute of the day. Many physical forms will discard this energy as trivial, however, our prayers can provide balance to the universe just by sending the given energy with the prayer. I do propose that by offering a sacrifice of something, be it smoke, or carved wood, tobacco, alcohol, or food stuffs, the willingness of surrendering the item produces an increase in energy provided. The additional focus of our intrinsic energy helps restore the balance within the universe from those who simply draw from the universe.

Worship

Like the rebranding of Seiðr magic into a practice called prayer, worship became the modern, culturally sensitive translation for the use of what used to be Galðr magic combined with the demonstrative value of the ritual. The underlying premise of worship is two-fold: one is the gathering of additional bodies, and therefore energy applied toward the completion of whatever request, and the second is frequency vibrations (or voices lifted in song), allowing for alignment with other spiritual entities. These two functions, once performed in rituals and other gatherings, were the prelude to the modern practice capturing the effectiveness to continue the progress for their practitioners. This is where we add the exponential addition of universal energy toward the completion of some tasks. We will discuss more about the evolution of practices that would ultimately evolve into what the new church referred to as worship in rituals.

Magic

We arrive at the point where we need to understand the influence on modern practices that magic of the time would have had. What exactly is meant when we talk about magic? Well, there are lots of definitions, and lots of types of magic, but as mentioned earlier, there isn't any real difference between the ancient form of magic and the current form of prayer. However, at its most basic core definition, it is vocalizing our request to the spiritual and the deities who are listening. We vocalize our request to employ the spiritual forces to begin the necessary energies to "nudge" all the required factors into place to ensure that we (the entity who initialized their prayer/magic) simply walk into the successful accomplishment of our life path.

I'd like to take a moment to call out some basic truths the early practitioners considered. The first, and more compelling portion to recognize, is that these early architects realized the power of magic. That it was a quantifiable thing that needed to be included in their

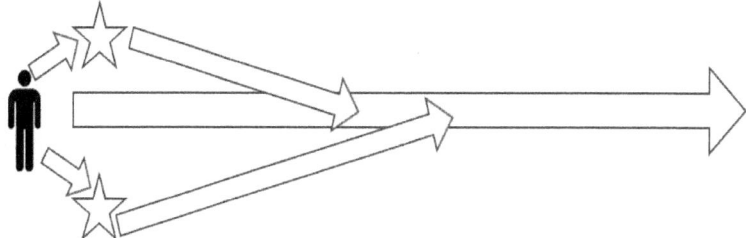

Figure 25 - *Incantation of magic or prayer is the same premise.*

developing practice. They recognized that not only did magic work, but when individuals believed (as most did) the magic became more powerful. While the general population did not understand the mystical power of the day and relied on shamans or druids to assist them, there was no doubt that the magic, when supported by the right energies, could accomplish whatever they needed. This is critical to understand when attempting to consider what we believe.

So, diving down past the surface connotations that many apply to the idea of magic into an understanding of how it all works. The use of Seiðr magic is a simple incantation of a spell (or request) with more than likely some practiced ritual surrounding the incantation process. This process then broadcasts the request to the spiritual realm, where both spirits and deities are monitoring based on the frequency of the aura presenting the request. Many factors become an influence after the spell/prayer has been initiated. This includes:

1. Our intention as to how badly we want it, and if our heart is into this spell/prayer for the right reasons. Those reasons are completely intrinsic. Our intention will also include our willingness to "stay with it" by constantly feeding it our intrinsic energies (either consciously or not).
2. The alignment to what others may have already incanted with a particular level of intention, and even what the deities desire in some cases. Obviously, if one achieves favor from the deities,

then their application of energy can conquer all other requests.
3. Our free will, as this tends to alter some requests before they come to fruition. Incanted spells or prayers do not transfer over to our new trajectory when we decide to change it, therefore will need to be re-incanted once on the new trajectory.

Many factors come into consideration when discussing the fruition of spells and prayers. It all boils down to the modern-day prayer being the same thing the Seiðr magic spell was when my ancestors roamed the physical plane. What many don't understand about their idea of prayer is that an incredibly select few requests poised to the universe in either magic spells or prayers are completed by deity level individuals, as more often it is completed by spiritual entities using the power of suggestion on other physical entities to complete the task.

In a previous chapter, we discussed the principle of assistive energies. In this, others throughout the chain of interactivity necessary to complete a universal task provide supportive energy to our request. In some cases, some of our actions are suggested by spiritual entities around us. This assists in bringing someone else's prayer/spell to fruition. In much the same way as outlined before, those instances when we become the necessary resource for completing another's prayer/spell alter our trajectory in our physical lifetime.

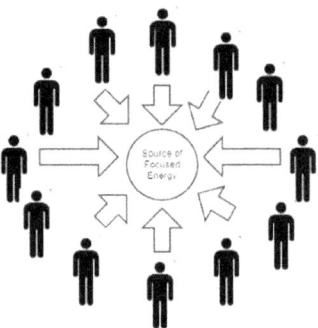

Figure 26 - *With more energy sources joined in focus, more energy is transferred to the request.*

These suggestions may provide the additional energy we need to complete the task but may also drain our energies from maintaining our level of intent on spells/prayers we have incanted. This is where processes such as everyday affirmations can maintain the intent on our prayers/spells, while draining one or two days to provide this resource for other physical entities around us.

Many within most modern-day practices apply negative connotations to the word and concept of magic, immediately assuming it's the "magic we see on television" or the evil magic of the movie industry. That is so far from the truth, it couldn't be any more opposite if they tried. Magic and spiritual energy does not possess evil or good powers, it is simply energy to be utilized for accomplishing tasks. The assignment of judgements such as "good or bad" can only be laid upon the issuer of said spell/prayer, as it is their intent (heart) that will drive what the energy is used for.

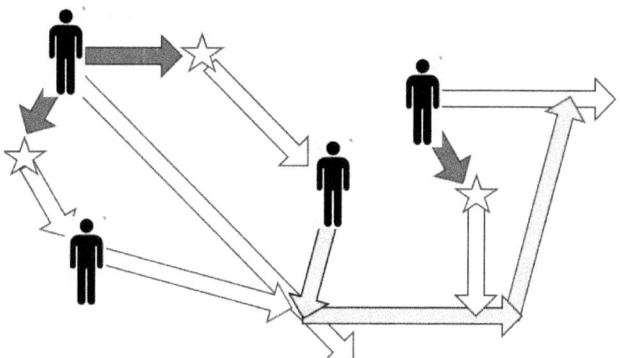

Figure 27 – *Every day we find ourselves as an energy source for other's prayers/spells.*

In much the same way, we could use the analogy of nuclear power. While in most cases it is used to power massive generators or ships at sea, it was also used in weaponry of the military. Similarly, magic is neither good nor bad; however, it can be used for good or bad purposes by an individual's intent.

Rituals

We find throughout recorded history evidence of spiritual rituals. These rituals range from the most secretive to the most lavish, and all points in between to demonstrate to the spiritual realm that there was a higher level of importance being placed on certain requests. The level of seriousness within rituals rose with the gravity of the hoped-for outcome as the rituals needed to provide enough intent to the spiritual realm. A notable number of societies felt that the sacrifice of another life form was necessary, but often, things of value were sacrificed to demonstrate the intent of the issuer. In every walk of life, under every belief system, extremism has always played a part in societies' opinion of a particular practice. This was no different for the early spiritual rituals where blood sacrifices were perceived as the level of necessity for successful outcomes.

However, as a better means of understanding the underlying wisdom about performing a ritual, we need to look past the public display, deep into the reasons we use a ritual. In much the same way modern day worship recognizes two distinct reasons for performing it, so too do the rituals of the past. The first was to demonstrate the individual's intent by determining the level of engagement in the ritual. The second was additional persons (possibly) who could provide additional universal energy, ultimately assisting in the successful completion.

Neither I nor the Landvætti I have communicated with over the years recognize the elimination of another life form as an approved form of sacrifice, as this does not demonstrate the individual's intent or need for the completion of the request. However, it can be noted that these types of actions were formerly seen as a necessity.

Most often we find a prescribed method, or series of actions performed in association with song and dance, so the combination of Galðr magic (pleasing music and dance) within the ritual provided the foundation that would later become this practice called worship. This is the type of event we find most often throughout the indigenous peoples of the world, obviously with few exceptions. There were ultimately two different levels of ritual performed:

A) Individual or personal rituals. This level would have a personal or a family altar, and the request would be specific in nature, leaning toward a request for a family member or immediate circle of clansmen/women. Most rituals focused on providing some sacrifice to the gods and were technically used to focus the individual's intent on the spiritual entities charged with bringing the request to completion. This demonstrated the surrendering

of something of value for spiritual support in trade.
B) Group rituals. This level extended from small groups to the inclusion of a community or clan. Group rituals were typically for larger, community-based requests. For example, a group ritual may be performed prior to an expedition with the intent that all return home safely or that the clan experience victory in a larger battle. Group rituals could employ multiple magicians together to garner the additional magical energy to increase the potential for a successful outcome.

Most rituals are a series of dancing and incanting phrases in a voice that is pleasing to the ear and sacrificing items that are beneficial to the specific gods and spirits needed to complete the task. In many cases, food and drink were offered, so the spiritual entities recognized the request as having a higher importance. Many attempted to provide a spiritual beacon by providing an altar that was charged with items of spiritual origin. In the days of my ancestors, small altars were constructed with carved rocks or trees representing the letters of the runes and symbols of the gods.

Our Intent and Commitment

Throughout the section of spiritual understanding, and the use of magic, we have included discussion points about the necessary intent. Let us look more closely at the two parts of this concept of intent. Drilling down into this concept can be a slippery slope of misunderstanding due to the evolution of the definition of the word.

Originally, our intent was purely based around our measurement of intrinsic desire of completion, or how much we wanted it. This is due to the simplicity of our ancestors, who sought only those endeavors that resulted in an honorable lifetime. This means that the prayers they uttered, or spells cast on their behalf, were based on their lives of seeking honorable outcomes for the benefit of the clan. As time moved on and generations came and went, the sacrifice of this quest for honor was transformed by the influx of individuals willing to surrender honor in the quest for materialistic needs of the flesh. Whereas in the previous generations we see a strict adherence to the principles of honorable living, we find the later generations desiring items of materialistic value. I believe that many turned to this newer paradigm as many associated honor with glory, and when the glory was not as much in abundance, they needed other methods to acquire the same stature in society.

I also believe that the following generations were not as interested, and therefore not as skilled, in the art of war, which continued the cycle of materialistic gains being more important than honor. This is stereotyping, as there have been generations of individuals who recognized and understood the core principle of honor and retained it as the center of their existence. However, I believe that those honor-centered individuals became the minority.

The two facets of our intention define how we interact with the spiritual sources around us. First, to do so intentionally means that we are applying some of our personal self (commitment) to whatever task at hand. Think of our intention like a water tap, typically defaulting to the off position. When we are tasked to do something, there are two states: we want to or we don't. On or off. However, like the water tap, we can escalate the pressure until it meets the requirement necessary to accomplish the task. Whatever it is. There remain some who reflect the modern commercial faucet taps, where there is no middle ground, either on or off all the way. These individuals are referred to as *allr* (Old Norse meaning "all") due to being either all-in or all-out, and while psychological science attempts to classify them as bipolar, or some other disorder, I consider them to be conserving their energies for the tasks they choose to tackle. This is the conversation we need to consider when discussing our intent to see something to completion.

The other aspect of our intent is a little more difficult to quantify, as it really is where our heart is as far as "good or bad." While the energy that is transferred between individuals (either spiritual or not) is neither good nor bad, it is the intent of the individual receiving it that then establishes the polarity.

We need to focus on constantly seeking ways to find joy and happiness, peaceful co-existence, harmony, and tranquility with ourselves, our family, our community and society at large, as this truly is the benefit of spirituality.

Focusing our Energy

Another key facet to consider is our energy focus. Typically, our aura in its natural state is more of a glow, a diffused light bubbling with colors. When we want to pass energy to those supporting our prayer or spell, the energy becomes more of a focused beam. This is a unique understanding, in that the normal diffused glow of our aura isn't a centralized enough beam of light to support multiple layers of spiritual support between the incanting individual and the request. So, focus is necessary. This focusing of energies has been accomplished by the rituals and more exaggerated movements and efforts of the magicians. Therefore, upon arrival of the new church in many different areas of Europe, we find the new practitioners following the tradition of exaggerated activities to display their intent, and more importantly, focus their universal energy on the task requested. This was/is the primary function of rituals, and ultimately, worship type of practices, focusing the energy on the task or thing necessary.

Influence of Karma

While the universe attempts to remain in balance, we discover the concept of karma. Within one of the many world religions comes the term *karma*, which means action, work, or deed. For those who subscribe to that theology, the term also refers to a cognitive process of cause and effect. The cause being the intent and actions of an individual which influence the future of that individual, thereby satisfying the effect. Operating on the concept of an intention bank, it keeps record of good intents and deeds as well as bad intents and deeds, which is then returned to the individual at some future time. This concept has also been adopted in popular culture, in which the events which happen after a person's actions may be considered natural consequences.

There are many who subscribe to this concept, whether by religious practice or by secular means. I believe that there is a little more to this idea than meets the reader's eye. First and foremost, we must always remember that each of us possesses the potential to use our free will at any time to change our trajectory in life, therefore, should some spiritual entity be keeping track, they would have to continually adjust the karma to be applied onto the new trajectory, which doesn't feel right to me. However, I believe that for those who choose to follow the paths through life given by the fates, then yes, this boomerang effect of negative energies would have an adverse effect. I will also admit that sometimes I too have hoped for some negative effect on an entity who may have slighted me, however I have discovered that it was I who was carrying the burden of the slight and not the one who I perceived caused it. While in the service of our spiritual entities, we are always searching for ways to better communicate and harmonize with others. Sometimes life gives us lessons to learn. The key here is to learn the lesson and not concentrate on what happens to the other person.

In addition, we need to evaluate the word "intent" again within the scope of discussing karma. Intent resides in an individual's heart; however, it is projected onto one's aura as well. So, when considering the cause and effect of karma, one needs to consider what is in the heart of the individual. While we may feel slighted in some way, the aura's projection may not include anything about the situation at all. While I understand the release theory behind the belief in karma, the reality is, we have no way of knowing what the intent was from the other party, and therefore, no way of knowing how they will be affected.

Divination and Reasoning

While divination is a fancy word for "getting advice," there are many facets we need to consider when attempting to grasp the far-reaching boundaries of the physical plane. Divination is the use of spiritual entities to provide some type of advice for getting our lives back on the right path. Typically, this advice is provided using some sort of medium, whether it be reading of the runes or tarot cards or a multitude of other methods. Sometimes it is visions or dreams or just ideas that pop into our mind. These are all ways we can accept advice. One of the major pieces of advice I offer is that none of these mediums or knowledge transfers can predict the future. Many profess they can, but it is impossible to tell the future unless one is describing the paths laid out by the fates due to our ability to use free will. The future is being written as we live through it, therefore the best we can hope to acquire from these divination mediums is alternate choices we can make. Possibilities, if you will.

I personally rely on my interpretation of the runestones to provide me with a medium in which to have concrete evidence as to which way I should, or should not, go in my life. Not as much as the defined path to my future, more to an idea of "this is how it's going to happen if you don't change something." Deciding on the changes necessary and making the appropriate changes in my life still falls squarely on my shoulders, as well as the ramifications for those decisions, either way.

A lot of individuals have sought me out in hopes I could tell their futures with runestones or tarot cards. The issue I have, and explain to them, is that there is really no way of seeing the future, as our intrinsic ability to use free will creates change after change that is impossible to foresee. The future is not set, and your ultimate physical life's destiny is what you make of it. By using free will, we can alter our trajectory through our physical existence as often as we feel we need to. With different information comes the potential for different directions in life.

When discussing the potentiality outside our lives, we need to seriously consider the principles of our lives. The first principle to know is: Everything happens for a reason. Whether that reason is bilateral damage from something else happening, or whether it's intentional, the immediacy is not usually obvious. Suffice to say, we need to consider all aspects when determining why things happen. The most probable reason for events transpiring in our lives is to learn from. Whether our lesson is for the physical or spiritual self is usually not clear from the onset; however, we need to seek the lessons within our experiences to make us better versions of ourselves.

Degraded Spiritual Trust

Some have spoken about the violation of trust that physical beings have had with spiritual entities throughout the last couple of millennia. While this has some level of truth, the greatest gift is that of helping others. Therefore, while there has been a level of darkness and isolation throughout the spiritual realm, as we might recall, many spiritual entities offer suggestions and/or mental nudging, whether we have chosen to recognize it or not.

Our spiritual entities remain in constant communication with the other lifeforms on the physical plane, including the animal kingdom, the plant environment, even mother earth maintains a constant connection. As individuals throughout the world pray or utter spells, the spiritual realm remains busy attempting to fulfill these communication requests, whether known to the physical inhabitants or not.

I do believe, as more people are finding the truth of spirituality, that the increase in communications is notable, yet there remain many obstacles that humankind has put up that still limit the reach of spiritual telepathy. I do believe that more are needed to find the truth to restore the interactivity with the spiritual realm to what it once was, but the movement is on.

Crossing Realms of Existence

As mentioned in an earlier section, the idea of moving a material object between realms of existence is impossible, and quite honestly, impractical. Therefore, when we speak of moving things into our reality on the physical plane, we are describing a process of resource reallocation. In other words, the spiritual entities, using their understandings and their power of suggestion, simply align donors with recipients. By seeking out and discovering physical entities who have whatever materialistic or intellectual item one is seeking, the spiritual entities use their power of suggestion that this person is a worthy recipient.

Technically, there are no material items within the spiritual or deity realms, as these eternal entities are formless and therefore have no need for such items. As mentioned before, if an entity requests (using magic or prayers) something that doesn't exist in the physical realm, then a deity evaluates and determines whether the prayer/spell will be granted. This is not to detract from the gifts that many have brought to the physical plane with their inventions throughout the eons, this is just to say that to create "something from absolutely nothing" requires a deity with universal energy.

Summary

There are tons of books on the market that speak to the use of magic, and/or the use of prayers to accomplish what we want in our lives. Ultimately, this all boils down to our ability to focus our intrinsic universal energies to help our spiritual entities use their authority of suggestion to reallocate resources currently in existence.

The concept of creating our reality comes back to the idea that we employ our spiritual entities to help reallocate current resources to enter our life's path. This reassignment of a resource to another identity should align with the forward movement of one's journey.

Whether through physical lifeforms or having those lifeforms manipulate material items into our trajectory's path to acquire them, magic (whether calling it that, or calling it prayer) is simply the use of our personal aura to communicate our desires to the spiritual realm for assistance in completion.

EXERCISES

Chapter 5 – Seeking Answers From the Previous Chapter

1. **Why do I believe in a god? How do I know he/she/they are real?**

   While I believe that my gods do have faces and can assume physical form to interact with either; other humans and/or the environment, I am more interested in seeing the energy all around me. Each day, as I open my eyes and see life happening around me, I realize that the centers of universal energy are at work. As I look to the other physical life forms around me and feel the ancestors encouraging me forward, I am convinced that they are as real as I am. I believe in a supreme energy source every time I see the miracle of life created or leaving this plane.

2. **Do I feel fulfilled within my belief system as to what I understand? How?**

   For the first time in my life, I can say I absolutely do. From an intellectual, emotional, and spiritual perspective, I have answers to all my questions, some questions I didn't even realize I had. I now know the indigenous peoples of the world understood far more than the controls placed on the peoples of the world by a manipulative puppet master that would become modern-day religion.

3. **Do I believe every part of the religious teachings? Why?**

   Now, with my cultural Celtic spiritual teachings, there is no way to unknow what I have been taught, as evidence is presented to me every second of every day that I'm on the physical plane. My teachings include the constant need to seek harmony and peace yet defend that which I have accomplished. While seemingly a contradiction, my ancestors teach me to protect what's mine and what I accomplished yet surrender those things that have been given to me. This is really the premise that has led me to teach what they have taught me.

4. **Do I recognize the difference between practice and spirituality in myself? How?**

   I have been taught that the difference between practice and true spirituality is that instant where I demand, either intrinsically in my own mind, or extrinsically by demanding that others subscribe to the same understanding I have about spirituality. When I determine that an individual's journey leads them to a different perspective than mine, I have two choices. I can choose to inquire about this different perspective to learn and understand, or I can dig my heels in and demand that my perspective is the "right" one. The moment I move to the second option, I have crossed from the beauty of a universal spirituality to the ugliness of a practice.

5. **What do I believe about "after death"? Why?**

   I have been taught that we simply shed this physical form and return to our spiritual self. As we shed our physical self, we are welcomed by our ancestors who help us to learn those things that we may have missed during our physical existence. In a review of our physical lives, we are shown the indicators for change that we may have overlooked in the "heat of the moment" on earth. As we depart the physical self, so too do the chemical interactions within our physical senses that allow us to see wisdom and intellect that we couldn't with that interference.

6. **What do I believe about before birth? Why?**

   I have been taught that our spiritual entities were all created by collecting universal energy eons ago and have chosen to experience this physical life for the reason of learning the emotional control necessary to obtain empathy for our descendants. Because the basic premise of living in today's world is very different than it was during the time of our ancestors, we may choose to live physical lives several times throughout our existence.

Absorbing the Energy of This Knowledge

Contained within this chapter has probably been the most controversial portion of the whole book, and while many have contention with the contents, what if it were all true? What if this was the way I saw spirituality? Does it make me wrong or evil? Of course not, it simply means we're different. Our physical existences provide different perspectives based on many factors. We need to ask ourselves what if it is true, what if there are other perspectives to the entirety of the spiritual realm. Many times, and throughout all of history, humans have let their imagination get the better of them by creating a sometimes-irrational fear of the unknown. It was this irrational fear that led to the rise of the shaman and ultimately of a religious practice throughout the world. Many believe that the trip out of the physical form is a one-way trip with no way of returning with the facts. However, whether you call out to the Christian or Muslim god or not, makes no difference in your embracing the concept that spirituality is as unique as each physical lifeform.

If we were to visit the wilderness and gaze upon a beautiful mountain scene, looking northward, would that view be the same as someone viewing the same mountain from the north looking south? Of course not. Therefore, our spirituality should be viewed with the same intellectual understanding that, unless we are standing on exactly the same path on our journey, our perspectives will never be the same. The same is true in our understanding of other's interpretation of their spiritual realm.

Let us use this opportunity to deeply ponder several critical understandings.

1. What are other perspectives of my spiritual values? How?
2. In consideration of my beliefs, have I allowed myself to be bullied into thinking otherwise? Why?
3. Can I feel the energy of prayer and magic? When? What does it feel like?
4. When out in the public, have I tried to "feel" other's aura? What did it tell you?
5. How do you feel about knowing the major religions of the world assimilated the ancient practices of prayer and worship?

Adopting Successful Wisdom Using Meditation

Using meditation is the best method for incorporating new information into the processing center of our brain. It allows our heart and mind to concentrate on determining if the knowledge/wisdom gathered complements or contradicts what we already know or believe. Use your meditative time of this chapter to not concentrate on the questions so much as the general ideas behind prayer, magic spells, and worship.

During this chapter's exercise, I ask that you consider your own power source. In antiquity, there were two forms of magic (defined in the chapter). Which one do you feel more closely associated with? This is not a matter of damning prayer as a source of power, it is simply a different way to understand the capacity that each of us has for drawing and focusing our intrinsic energies.

Chapter Six

Interpretations of the Modern Day

The idea behind this book is not to convince anyone of anything they don't already believe, but to allow them to have a deeper understanding of *why* they believe what they do. The millennia-old issue of religious practices that have placed profits over true understandings undermined our idea of theology for many generations and made the quest for knowledge in spirituality taboo for many. My hope is that you do not change your beliefs until you've had a chance to fully investigate what your beliefs are at the most fundamental core level and determine what fits best by "feeling right", and "making sense", as these really are the cornerstones to our spirituality. In the same breath, when we discover our own intimate relationship with a spiritual association that meets the above criteria, we should no longer have an expectation that others are required to change theirs to match what we believe. We must always remember when it comes to our personal theology, there really are no wrong answers for anyone. Our hearts and minds will tell us what works for us, and with an infinite being above us, I am comfortable saying that he/she/they will be all right with that.

I believe that the more individuals who discover their true beliefs and fully understand the entirety of a beautiful, intimate relationship they have with their interpretation of a deity, while recognizing and embracing the associated spiritual influences, the more commonality we can all experience within our lives, which then leads to a peaceful co-existence with all peoples of all the lands. When the objective becomes how we can better the human experience here on the physical plane for everyone, and how we can evolve to the next level of physical life. I believe bringing more love to the center of our lives will be a critical component in making this lifetime a better experience for all who travel it.

Within the gifts we have of being a spiritual being at our core is the intrinsic ability to exercise our free will and completely change the trajectory of our lives at any time. This ability allows us to walk away from behavior that is unacceptable to either us or our community, at any time. We retain the power as well as the ability to alter our life's trajectory in any direction we choose, with the understanding that the emotional lessons on our new trajectory may be completely different and may produce some negative impacts that we will have to learn from. Altering our mindset to change behaviors, regardless of the situation, is always a possibility, as one needs to remember that our physical body is only ours until it fails.

I have found in my interactions with people that many have a disconnect of sorts between what is spiritual and what they consider everyday life. I hope the contents of this book have provided the real-world connection between the science and true spirituality as it exists. By thoroughly understanding the physical science behind the situation we find ourselves in, hopefully provides some lessons on how we can grasp the use of spirituality to better our experience in this lifetime.

Perception is Reality

All too often in this modern-day world of hurry up, we are content with only seeing the surface of most situations without expending additional resources to look more deeply into situations. I have told my children for as long as they have been alive that "perception is reality," or in other words, the way that many see the world is how they think it is, and most won't take the time to actually get to know the facts. In many cases, this should speak volumes as to the stored memory (or knowledge) within their minds. By only getting a small fraction of the overall truth, we are content and usually quickly change focus f and move on, satisfying the level of perception. This is what many use to build their understanding of life. Therefore, many have preconceived notions, thereby forming judgments based on a shallow level of understanding. The idea that many among the modern population have chosen to collect the data from the world around them only at the level of their perception and not any deeper, hopefully creates an understanding that most of these perceptions are completely inaccurate. For this reason, we should always validate the data we receive.

> *"Our wisdom may be more resistant to challenge when we know less more completely, than it is to know more at a surface level."*
>
> -Alaska Úlfhéðnar

Relationships created based on a superficial understanding establish a diminished level of total knowledge that some construe as wisdom. The unfortunate reality is that frequently, when one of the "base" memories of knowledge is determined by the self to be inaccurate, it creates the potential to cause a cascade of relationship failures that casts doubt on all the related memories as well. Therefore, in the quest to solidify what we really do know, we need to move beyond the superficial glances we receive and truly see the world the way it is intended to be seen. By understanding and validating each piece of our knowledge, we can establish a more firm foundation to establish our wisdom from. This should be the task we seek for every piece of understanding.

Willingness to Stand Alone

This is one of the topics that surfaces time and again. At our core, humans are social creatures, depending on strength in numbers as their necessary for survival. Most individuals I have interacted with over the years have always drawn a parallel between being a part of the church to the early evolution of humankind, where we relied on safety in numbers, so we were willing to surrender some of our individuality for the sake of safety or protection. The surrendering of our uniqueness should never be a part of the decision-making process. While we may be best suited to larger populations, the ability and willingness to stand against what's wrong or intolerable or what doesn't make sense should always be a tool we have and are willing to use.

The days are long gone where we depended on the safety in numbers philosophy, and therefore we need to start taking responsibility for our safety and the protection of what we have rightfully earned, as well as our independent thinking. While every attempt should be made to avoid violence in any form, there comes a time where negotiations will break down, and the protection of one's property or self must be taken in-hand physically. We should be willing to stand against the ill intent of others and not cower in favor of being protected by others. The idea about the text of this book is to provide an understanding for you to thoroughly understand your emotions, and your personal connection to the spiritual and deity realms, allowing you to believe what you believe without doubt or reservations. You should never rely on anyone else to determine what you believe. Remember, you are the master of your mind and your physical life. You need to take, and maintain, control of your spirituality and your emotional life.

Acceptance seems to be the most challenging of all the tasks based on generations of humans handing down practices instead of theology. Most mainstream religious practices have fought against this idea of acceptance for centuries, preaching the necessity to "save" people from eternal damnation and their idea of "hell." This has created the prescription for the death of many cultures and many more within those cultures throughout the history of the monotheistic practice. The idea of acceptance without expectation of obedience, or the tolerance of other belief systems, especially in contradiction to their own, has eluded some monotheistic practices for as long as they have existed. To this point, we need to make a concentrated effort to understand that having a different relationship with our unique interpretation of a deity figure is central to our unification. Moving away from the definition of "tolerance" to the concept of "acceptance" establishes a different mindset. Being different provides us with a perspective that should demonstrate the awesomeness of our deity, or deities.

I encourage everyone to understand that spiritual beliefs should be unique and individual to each person. If an individual chooses to seek new information, and that information feels right in their heart, makes sense in their minds, then they should follow whatever fulfills them. However, the enforced practices of the monotheistic churches have led to more rebellion and formation of additional branches, as well as counter-branches, which then led to a vicious circle of death and continued enforcement. This cycle must stop for humankind to reach its potential. It is only when we find peace in our spirituality that we can begin our journey toward empathetic life and enlightenment.

After taking an intrinsic inventory of our personal beliefs, we must then remove judgement from our assessment of others, as they will have a very different relationship with their deity than we have with ours. Sometimes it's easier to say someone else is wrong or incorrect in their beliefs, whereas we come from a position of indifference to our own beliefs. This mentality has led to the misunderstandings and misrepresentations that have been passed through generations. This has caused a constant influx of damage to individuals on both sides of the relationship since the very beginning.

Understanding the Self

When considering the understanding of oneself, one needs to consider both the physical entity as well as the spiritual one, as both are required to accomplish balance. We can start by taking an intrinsic inventory of our personal theological beliefs and spiritual understandings. Given the current societal influence, this can be very challenging as we need to address the separation between the theology and the practices.

What if those things we've talked about in the practice of monotheism are not correct? What if the god that monotheists worship is the same as one of my gods? What if you knew that prayers and incanted magic spells were the same thing? These are all serious questions we need to understand. If you stopped for just a minute to consider that our deity is an infinite being and could easily incorporate all these different interpretations into his/her/their being, would that make you believe or think differently? Understanding that all these different beliefs are not wrong just because we don't see each other on Sunday morning is a cornerstone to letting some of these practices go. Many struggle to understand the difference between theology and an accompanying practice. While I will not dictate your spiritual or theological beliefs, I can say something about what you should look for within yourself to help understand your own.

Our theology should be comfortable and make sense to us. When considering our underlying theology, we should not need a book to understand it. I would like to remind us all that no two intimate relationships with a deity (theology) should be exactly the same. With the number of genetic differences, chemical mixtures which caused certain sensory inputs to be stored in your brain as knowledge, we shouldn't concern ourselves with what others believe unless we find that we are not feeling fulfilled by what we believe. That's not to say that if someone gives you information (like I have in this book) and it makes sense to you in your mind and feels right in your heart, then maybe looking more closely into the study is acceptable, but it needs to be on your terms.

Obtaining Balance in our Life

Another lesson we must seek to accomplish is to identify and obtain a level of balance in our life. This is about obtaining a balance between our spiritual selves and our physical self, performing the actions necessary for the display and energy of intent, while at the same time reaching out to the spiritual realm with requests for events or information. After a discussion of prayers and spells, followed by our physical actions of seeking in equal parts, we begin to obtain balance between the realms. Balance is obtained between asking for our deities' help and performing the action steps, establishing avenues for the deity to provide opportunity. This is really the understanding that each part of our entity cannot function as well without the other. For as long as we inhabit a physical body, we must seek to balance our physical actions with our spiritually driven wants and needs to find true success. A critical piece to obtaining our spiritual wants and needs is focusing on how to co-exist with other interpretations, as spiritual entities recognize the value of harmony.

In the days of my ancestors, most tasks were handled by the physical entities, while spiritual influences were reserved for the more serious and potentially unmovable things, like weather and the fates. While one might assume the balance was tilted the other way, leaning more toward the physical beings handling most, if not all, without the interference of a deity or spiritual source. However, when our ancestors called on their interpretation of the deities or called upon a Seidr magician to incant spells to alert the spiritual entities, it was for tasks much grander in scope. So, ultimately the balance was maintained.

When we seek balance in our life, t it is perfectly acceptable to hope and to pray. These spiritual processes must be accompanied by a physical action. Those physical actions could be to create daily affirmations that we repeat, thereby generating the intrinsic intent for the provision of energy. It could be, as I've said before, an obstacle that we've placed such as praying for a million dollars but not buying a lottery ticket. If the same prayer (a million dollars) was uttered while deep within the uncharted lands of the earth, this comes down to creating something from nothing, and therefore requires a deity to be involved. At this level, we must project a lot more cosmic energy into the spiritual realm to summon a deity's attention. However, for the lion's share of our requests from our spiritual entities, they (our spiritual connections) will be able to utilize the power of suggestion to re-allocate the necessary resources. We simply must desire it enough without placing any mental obstacles in the way.

Change Brings Fear

Many people are terrified of changes in their life. Some even fear a change within the influence on their lives. Change is inevitable, and therefore should be embraced instead of being feared. Norse legends offer the idea that our lives are guided by a group of spiritual entities referred to as the Fates, or Moirai. This path was simplistic in nature, typically avoiding any emotional swings from extreme to extreme, simply following with a policy of acceptance, meeting the low bar requirements for emotional understanding. While this path grants the individual the emotional experiences necessary to successfully navigate a physical existence, that's all it does. Today, we refer to this as a victim mentality. While most victims I've worked with have used the dark energy of the universe to kill off this mentality and power themselves forward, others remain trapped in this thinking. One might wonder, how does one change one's trajectory?

A large part of changing our trajectory is realizing that the power to change is intrinsic. No amount of counseling can force us to realize that. By changing our mindset to being in the driver's seat, or in command, one creates the opportunity to break the cycle of allowing the victim mentality to occupy our minds.

Living our lives on our terms and exercising our ability to use our free will offers a life more fraught with emotional ups and downs that will take its toll on us but is ultimately more fulfilling. In addition, this path provides the most emotional intellect, thereby setting our spiritual self up for successful navigation of our spiritual existence after this physical one is left behind. By altering our mindset to being responsible and living intentionally, we can begin the process of taking back control. This is the idea of "the self." This was the underlying reason our ancestors were as successful as they were. No one was going to do the task for them, so they had to buckle down and get it done. It is a paradigm shift from most of today's thinking, but we see evidence all around us of it working as it's supposed to.

The idea behind this section is really understanding one of the major differences between modern humans and our ancestors. Without the systems in place, our ancestors were convinced of, and ready and willing to do what was necessary to accomplish whatever they needed without the help of deities or spirits. They lived their lives their own way and took a commanding role in the trajectory of their lives. This allowed for a lifetime of simplicity. This intention meant that they knew what needed to be done in their lives and did it.

This is a large contingent in the forces necessary to alter our trajectory in this life. We need to want it. We need to perform the physical tasks necessary. Just as importantly, we need to convince ourselves that we should, and we can, do this. While many struggle here, I am convinced that the spiritual forces at work around us will support and collaborate with us to make these changes. Being willing to live our own path will catapult our success.

In the ancient Norse traditions, there were stories of three sisters, called the Nornir sisters, sometimes referred to as the Fates. Each sister had a role to play in our physical existence. The traditions and stories of the sisters morphed as the stories traveled. however, in the earlier Germanic (Celtic) understandings, there were:

"Atropos was the oldest sister, and she determined the length of one's life upon the bonding of spirit to physical body. Lachesis was the sister who determined in which great hall an individual would reside after leaving the physical body. She determined which hall based on the tapestry sewn by her sister Clotho. The tapestry sewn by Clotho included the details of one's physical life and how closely one abided by the nine noble virtues."
-Ancient Germanic Tribe tradition

The stories of the sisters and our ultimate destination brought forth this idea of the tapestry of our life's deeds. This idea was rebranded with the modern religious practices as Judgment Day, where we took accountability for the tasks and deeds we had committed throughout our physical lifetime. However, for some, it took on a different meaning. In my case, I view my tapestry as something that I alone am responsible for weaving. Not as an author putting pen to paper, but by my actions and intentions. Looking at my tapestry as a third-party reporting of my life, the responsibility is in my hands to make right. Our tapestry could be written by allowing things to happen to us or by the selves making things happen for us. The choice is ours.

Understanding Societal Impact

One of the first ideas that we need to clear from our processing is the idea that being different is wrong. Although that stigma seems to be less of a threat today than it was a decade ago, the underlying shame and guilt are still applied with just as much psychological impact. The era of practice enforcement has long passed its useful life cycle and needs to be replaced with an understanding as to what we need to do to understand our selves and our relationships with the spiritual realm. The negative connotations that have been applied to the many practices outside of the mainstream religions have had lethal ramifications throughout the history of the church and continue to force conflict in many nations and communities in the world today. The tactic that these practices have used of peer pressure and public shaming (intentional or not) has created conflict in the modern world. The added burden of guilt or shame that many have been forced to carry for performing whatever was necessary to survive honorably has caused an abyss within the heart and spirit of individuals. In some cases, we have witnessed an overwhelming shadow caused by these tactics that led to a significant increase in the level of depression, creating a cycle of shame and guilt that many feel they cannot escape from. However, there is hope. There is a way to escape the guilt/shame cycle, even if you choose to believe in the theology of these practices.

One of the most overlooked aspects of spirituality is the effect the connection to the spiritual realm has on our everyday psychology. With the ability to undermine what we think we know, the spiritual realm needs to be seriously considered when we ponder why we believe what we do. By obtaining a level of emotional control and by carefully evaluating spiritual connections, we set ourselves up for success by addressing them up front. Being proactive in our spirituality allows us better understandings of the messages conveyed from other spiritual sources. Ridding our minds of emotionally charged memories gives us a clear mental state for added clarity from our spiritual communications received. These ideas go to the heart of living our lives intentionally. We must intentionally remove the emotional landmines that have been placed in our psyche, either by guilt or shame.

If we find that we are uncomfortable or struggle with understanding our spiritual connections, seek out individuals who do not have a subliminal agenda to provide you with basic understandings. Know in your heart that you are still going to have to do the work of translating these basic interpretations into your life. A shaman can offer you a map of the area, but you need to do the walking. You now know of the requirement for physical activity, as well as the intent, therefore, hopefully you understand that we have two choices in life:

1) Follow the path laid out for us by the fates, including an emotional existence. Not really an experience, just an existence. Today, as mentioned before, we call this a victim mentality and assume that the individual is simply passing off the accountability and responsibility for commanding their own mind.
2) We can take charge of our destiny by making choices to experience the emotional rollercoaster this existence offers. While this path may result in painful ramifications, the desire is to gain emotional experience and learn a level of control to prepare us to return to the spiritual realm upon the demise of our physical body.

While we may hear a message of peace and co-existence from the practitioners of the mainstream religions, the base doctrine dictates that any person outside of these beliefs is condemned to their idea of a horrible fate, creating an intrinsic perceived need of the inadvertent practitioner to "save" or convert any outsider to their practice. A natural reaction by caring individuals who wish to save others from this horrible fate, which is commendable, but incorrect in its application. There have been too many examples where individuals have taken this to the extreme by either converting or killing those who are different in their beliefs for fear of them living life in their perceived understanding of sin. Sin is the indoctrinated understanding of good versus bad within a particular practice. It is someone's interpretation of what is good for humankind. This has caused the death of more cultures than any germ, gun, or steel ever released throughout history. Ultimately, we need to understand that every living thing has an intimate relationship with their deity or deities, and more emphasis should be placed on the individual's benefit to the community in lieu of some perceived label of their theology.

We all need to take a breath and learn the major lessons of life to establish our emotional control. By stepping back in our minds and not correcting everyone else's behavior, only continuing to learn and grow and find like-minded individuals, we can begin to change the world.

One of the major threads that I hear when discussing this with those who have separated from the mainstream teachings is the idea that "they (the church) can't change beliefs, they can only enforce obedience to their practice". This is 100% true. While we can offer suggestions, ultimately the decision comes down to the individual as to what they believe. Anyone can punish someone long enough to enforce obedience, however, it does not change their underlying belief. I believe that many find themselves in this camp. Forced to obey the social rules placed by society or families, yet struggling with believing anything of the doctrine. I feel as if the millions of people around the world changing their "practice" are really searching for their beliefs.

Applying Simplicity to Our Daily Lives

One of the major keys that our ancestors enjoyed is simplicity. While their lives may have been filled with a very localized level of dramatic events. This level of simplicity allowed them to focus on more important pursuits. Their destinies were more pronounced with this level of simplicity; however, this can be accomplished in modern day life as well. My first recommendation would be to turn off the news. I know my stress level elevates whenever I catch glimpses of the news on TV or my computer. Our spiritual and mental health is a higher priority than anything else. As a society, we need to place less value on demonstrative material gains and more on spiritual enlightenment, as the quest for material wealth has always produced a level of measurable stress and angst within ourselves. Be content with the sights and sounds of nature, seek other's company as friends and not as comparisons. These are truly the best ways to acquire simplicity.

One of the major forms of stress is division, as it is not our natural state. While the stress of society does provide emotional instability, giving rise to the educational purpose of our time here, the lessons can be learned in other ways. As spiritual entities, we should always strive to care for our fellow life form here on earth and accept our differences, as it is truly what makes our time here more pleasant.

Discovering and Accepting Our Theology

Beneath the pretense of modern-day practices lies the intimate relationship that we experience with our unique interpretation of our deity or deities. That relationship is the most private of all our relationships, as it is the underpinnings of the experiences we have with our spouses, our children, even our parents. However, many throughout history have tried to enforce their ideas of what our religion should look and even feel like. This is the reason I wrote this book. To find peace and harmony within our lives, we must discover our own theology, and while condemning relationships that are counter-productive to our society, we must discover and accept our own relationship with our deity, or our theology, not to cause division, but to better understand others' relationships to their deities, thereby fostering understanding and hence, unification. To discover our relationship, we need to use our physical sensory input to generate enough emotion to feel if this understanding is a correct fit for us. In addition, we must use the stored data within our brain, our knowledge, to determine if our theology makes sense to our beliefs.

Sometimes different aspects feel right and make sense, while other aspects don't. We need to be unafraid of changes and willing to exercise our free will to alter our trajectory. We always have that power. Each of us needs to seek the guidance and understanding offered by our spiritual connections, as well as our deities in the quest for establishing peace with all peoples regardless of their beliefs.

While we seek our spirituality, we must remember that one of the cornerstones of our beliefs should include principles as to how we accept others and their beliefs and interpretations. While our relationships with our deities should be individual, the collaboration with others to make our physical existence more comfortable should always be sought. As mentioned earlier, the more individuals who contribute energy toward a common goal, the more probable the successful outcome will be. Sharing one's beliefs is a gift, but understanding that others may have different beliefs allows for the flourishing of all beliefs, and that it's perfectly acceptable to be different.

A New Form of Practice

When considering how the information within this book will change your life, one needs to seriously contemplate the information you have just read. As a spiritual being within a physical body, utilizing the physical sensory input into the brain through the concoction of chemical composition that leads to whatever you took away, one needs to ask, "Does this make sense?" Do the ideas throughout this book feel right? These are truths that we need to discover for ourselves. Just as importantly, no two physical entities are going to interpret ideas the same way and be willing to accept this truth. We need to deploy a level of compassion for our fellow humans. Just because someone thinks differently as they work to understand their interpretation, or feel differently about their levels of spirituality, doesn't make them wrong, or less right, it only adds to the beauty of differences. Individual journeys need to be educated and not judged. While one is free to inform others of their beliefs, as I've done with this book, it doesn't mean this is *the way*. It is simply *a* way. The text within this book contains the message I received from the Landvætti, then interpreted through my chemical composition. I hope that I have given you the information necessary for you to embark on your own journey of discovery.

As we begin to search through our spiritual beliefs and understandings, we should come away with the idea that, beyond the practices of modern religions, spiritual beliefs are where we find commonality among all the entities of the physical plane. There isn't any evil in the spiritual entities. We can help the intentions of others as they seek peace, joy, and co-existence with their spirituality in lieu of the practice of being more right than any other spiritual practice. We are all accurate in what we believe in spiritually, and if our beliefs give us peace, joy, and harmony with others, then it really shouldn't matter what religious affiliation we want to believe in.

Hopefully, you come away from this book with the knowledge that your existence here is for your emotional education and ultimate understanding of empathy. It is important to see the many practices for what they are: control mechanisms that have far outlived their usefulness. Separate your honest beliefs to include whatever theology you want to subscribe to, that is to be used for the comfort and cooperation among all the peoples throughout this plane of existence. This is then something we can all feel comfortable supporting and believing in.

So, putting a little "rubber on the road" here, let's start with some ideas as to how we can get stability within our personal aura. We need to consider the major contributing factor in the projection of our aura to the spiritual realm: our emotional state. By working through different exercises, we can clear hidden emotional memories in the brain, minimizing the fluctuations in our aura. For now, we know that with the influence of chemical interactions on our sensory input, we can alter the knowledge absorbed during that time. In much the same way, the emotional instability transmitted to the aura is affected, thereby misrepresenting our transmission and/or corrupting the information received from our spiritual entities and deities. With this knowledge, we can see the value of maintaining our emotional state.

Finding Your Inner Spirituality

The next section contains exercises to know our spiritual beliefs. Our spirituality is directly connected to our physical sensory input, so it is not unheard of to hear different things, see vignettes, or even smell something weird during these questioning periods. Because the ears are listening and the brain processing, the sensory input provided will transmit directly to the heart, which may release the "excitement" hormones into the bloodstream.

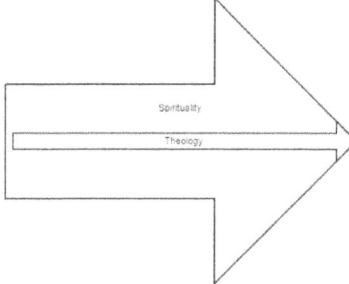

Figure 28 - *Our theology is a small portion of our overall spirituality.*

Our theology is only a fraction of our overall spirituality. There are a multitude of sources that we can communicate with and should be listening to in order to increase our clarity and potential for understanding. However, our deity is only a small portion of our overall spirituality. Including our spiritual entities in our prayers and incanted spells may offer a faster perceived resolution to our request. Associating with our ancestry helps in that we can safely assume that they have a similar genetic and chemical construct, thereby being able to understand our situation.

The emotional state management is incredibly important. In one of the last sections of the book are several exercises to help you understand what you think you believe and what your heart tells you that you really do.

There are a couple of key components to the success of these exercises, but probably the most important is your ability to be honest with yourself to determine where you are spiritually. Obviously, only you will know the results; however, the truth of one's discoveries has been projected to the spiritual realm for some time, which may explain your lack of success in prayers and/or spells cast. Both deities and spiritual entities do not want to be associated with insincerity or fakes. This exercise is for you to understand your spiritual connection on the spiritual plane, as well to understand your definition of a deity. You would do well to treat this relationship better than a physical being.

Ridding our memories of emotional charges will affect the projection of our aura. Understanding our personal theology and what we really believe is critically important to our personal fulfillment. Ultimately, this is our objective in uncovering smaller emotional charges hidden throughout the mind.

There are two parts. The first part is questioning each section of our intrinsic beliefs. The second part is that as we focus our attention on different sections, we should have some emotional interaction. This is really where we begin to listen with our heart. Our brain dissects the belief into segments to test, and our heart tells us which segment is legit as it responds with an emotional attachment to that memory, producing a negative, positive, or neutral position. A neutral position should be seriously considered, as our core theology should produce a joyful feeling of contentment.

Ultimately, at the end of the day, our theology should never include how we, or others, behave toward our deity. Our beliefs are no different than how we would or should treat our significant other. Theology is an understanding of a deity figure and our relationship with that figure. It does not include how others will have a relationship with a deity.

Our theology is our intimate relationship with a deity. My relationship with my deities is not your relationship. Even if you want to subscribe to my cultural beliefs in what I see as my personal relationship with my deities, your perspective and your genetic chemistry create a difference between us, and that is totally acceptable. It has nothing to do with the correctness of others or the behavior we exhibit either during some type of ritual or just being in society. Theology is purely a deity thing, and everything else is the practice.

EXERCISES

Chapter 6: Seeking Answers From The Previous Chapter

1. **What are some other perspectives of my spiritual values? How?**

   I have many friends who only see one god, and they are good with that. I recognize that their vision of only one deity represents the ease with which they function and find comfort. I have friends who don't recognize a deity figure at all, but rather a collection of spiritual energies around us, and that too, is perfect. Neither of these groups are incorrect in their view of the life force of the world. My spiritual values include the recognition of other's interpretation of the universal energies.

2. **In consideration of my beliefs, have I allowed myself to be bullied into thinking otherwise? Why?**

   For many years, I questioned what I thought I knew. I sought and received training as a minister of a Christian church. I clearly remember times when I could have said that I was bullied into believing something, even though I had no proof, and it really didn't feel right. But, as the gods have explained, human's need for a certainty or clear path led me to the place where I was concerned for my eternal peace. Again, I believe I allowed this bullying because I was fearful of what lie beyond the physical lifetime.

3. **Can I feel the energy of prayer and magic? When? What does it feel like?**

   I can feel the energy and power of prayer and magic in almost every aspect of my life. Sometimes I feel pulled in a different direction and wonder if my wife's prayers are guiding me. Other times, the guttural power of wanting something or someone to an action is tangible in my body. I feel this frequently when the wind gently pushes me one way or the other, or the sea calls out to me. Sometimes it's a phone call from someone who just wants to talk. There are many ways to "feel" when you are sending or receiving the energy of prayers or magic incantations.

4. **When out in the public, have I tried to "feel" other's aura? What did it tell me?**

   Frequently, when I am out in public, I am affected by the auras of the individuals around me. Trips through heavily populated areas can feel like an emotional paint can shaker, jarring my spirit with sads, and angers, happiness, and joys, all in a matter of several feet. Many times, large crowds exhaust me. The messages I received from these visits typically allow me to understand an individual's needs. Sometimes, the message is very convoluted, other times clear as day. It usually takes a day to process everything.

5. **How do you feel about knowing the major religions of the world assimilated the ancient practices of prayer and worship?**

   I am asked this frequently, and my answer is always the same. I feel wonderful about it, because those practices work! Throughout time, men and women have discovered a method of communicating with the spiritual world. They discovered early in our ancestry that you are the power source that makes the world move. Each of us powers our way through life's experiences in search of the ultimate source and understanding of empathy. Therefore, it is absolutely wonderful that all humans can rejoice in their ideas and understandings of their spiritual connections and celebrate it openly.

Absorbing the Energy of This Knowledge

In this section, we talked about going forward in our physical existence after being exposed to the knowledge in this book. There are ultimately two paths we can choose, as discussed in the text:

1. We can discard this new information and keep living the way we were. We can maintain our constant puzzlement on where power comes from and be surprised when something in our

world happens.
2. We can absorb this information and spend time learning what it is that we really think we know. We can accept the responsibility for being in control of our destiny, understanding that we may make mistakes, but that each of those mistakes is an opportunity to learn something new.

Adopting Successful Wisdom Using Meditation

We have covered a substantial number of topics to meditate on. At this point, I would like to offer one final topic to focus on during a meditation session:

Nothing

That's right, nothing. Let your mind wander through the spiritual universe and discover what it shows you, and more importantly, teaches you about your beliefs and your life in general. Remember, what you seek you will find, so during each of your meditations, seek peace and harmony.

Chapter Seven

Why I Wrote This Book

This book was written to explain the ideas and understandings that I have received from my spiritual channeling about the triad that exists within the human experience. As I have traveled my path of existence, I struggled with understanding those "abnormalities" that occur throughout life, especially given the amount of spiritual interactivity I have experienced. I've noticed within my own mind where associations between different memories are made that don't seem to make sense when I consciously think about them, but in some cases, as I continue to gain more knowledge about the subject, the pieces begin to fall into place and my understanding becomes much broader. However, it has only been through hindsight that this became apparent. Therefore, I offer this information that I sought and received about this unique condition. Because we each come from unique perspectives, I have been encouraged to explain the whole process in as much detail as I have been taught.

The Triad

The triad is how our mind attempts to make sense of everything I've given you in terms of how we may or may not receive information. Our experiences are stored as individual memory pieces in different locations throughout the brain, after being bathed in a hormonal shower throughout the process of input to storage. These memory bits are then related to other memory bits using either other physical sensory input (i.e., we heard the event, we visually witnessed), or in some cases the link between memory bits can be fulfilled by data received via a spiritual source, or deity source.

Many have taught me that the memory bits in our mind relate to other memory bits when we use an experience to relate the two bits. In other words, we are taught something, then we experience it. Upon experiencing it, we connect one memory to another related, or related contradictory memory, within our minds. This relation building becomes wisdom. As more and more memory bits become related, the sense of wisdom becomes larger and more profound. These experiences may be provided by either living the experience or it is given by our spiritual entities who pass information to the physical world.

Therefore, the understanding that our psychology may be altered by some spiritual interactivity, and the science as to how that happens, completes what I refer to as our individual triad of understanding. As you may recall in the previous chapters, I have referred to us (humans) needing to feel good about a belief, as well as have it make sense in our minds. This triad is how this comes together. We know intrinsically what feels right, however, many have inquired about the scientific portions for them to help make sense of it all. Hopefully, this book has given you some idea as to how our interpretation of spirituality and theology may directly alter our psychology and how those changes in psychology could alter our base DNA, changing us as physical entities. The intent of this book is to provide you with enough scientific information to help your brain make sense of what your heart has known all along, that you are right in what you believe.

Where do we go from here?

While I may have produced a lot of information within the pages of this book, my hope and desire are that you use this information to begin the process of understanding your unique perspective of the relationship that exists between you and your deity(s) and you and your spiritual entities. I do not wish you to change your core beliefs (or convert you) without you knowing what your beliefs are. Only you know you.

I hope you understand that there really is no right or wrong answer within our spiritual beliefs. We must seek peace and harmony with every entity, regardless of whether that entity is a member of the plant world, the animal kingdom, or a fellow human being. The fact remains, they too are seeking emotional intellect at some level. While the journey that our spiritual self has chosen may have experiences of pain and discomfort, they are lessons to be learned that will bring us to a place where we can fully embrace empathy.

The facts contained within the universal truth bear witness to the reality of where our spiritual understandings should focus. This truth crosses all the perceived lines of separation and division to connect us together at the deepest of levels. Whether we choose to acknowledge our ancestors or not does not change that they are here, but we are using our eyes to search for them when we should use our heart. We spoke of exercise methods of mindfulness to focus on what makes our heart feel joy and love.

Within the text that I have presented here is the message that hate and division are not a part of the natural order of things and are typically the product of uncontrolled egos, as is any form of supremacy, whether it be by sex, skin color, even disability. Within the spiritual realm, we are all formless collections of energies, equal in every way. The spiritual entities that enjoy our company only seek unification and joy and most importantly, love.

We should now recognize that the message we receive from our spiritual entities cannot be evil, but it is through our intent that the energy is polarized one way or the other. We must clearly understand where our heart, and more importantly, our intent, lies. By seeking to implement the nine noble virtues into our everyday life, we can expect that any darkness in our lives will be lifted, replaced by the everlasting light of love. We should spend more time working on our intimate relationship with our deity. Be one with them.

Throughout the pages of this book, I have revealed the idea of understanding our spiritual sensory input. We now know that sometimes when we get those feelings, glimpses, or even sounds that cannot be otherwise defined or validated, our spiritual entities may be attempting to communicate with or through us. We need to listen to the message not with our ears, but with our heart. We also now know that they have been communicating with us our entire physical existence, therefore we need to evaluate what we think we know to determine how much we know resonates in the heart as communications from these spiritual entities. The after effect of the chemical interactions that our bodies produce naturally are to help us learn and grow, so ensuring that the data we have in our mind can be validated by the heart is a critical component to reaching our spirituality.

Remember to live intentionally. By saying what we mean and meaning what we say. we begin to ensure that we become the masters of our physical body and mind. By being more mindful to what we store in memory, and what we project through our spiritual aura, we can increase the clarity of the messages we receive, while at the same time, increasing the energy applied to our prayers or spells.

We now know that magic is real and that the modern use of prayer is the exact same thing. By incanting our desires, applying our intent, focusing our energies, we are more probable in getting a successful outcome. We also know that praying for others creates a higher energy transmission than if we pray for ourselves, for the basic understanding of the gift is higher than the self.

All that aside, we need to clean house. We need to go through our mind and isolate our memories to discover which memory bits no longer apply, or if they are the emotional timebombs that will wreak havoc on our aura, then we can face them to remove them permanently. There will be memory pieces that may cause us discomfort and pain as they are addressed; however, by facing them, the pain is short lived then resolved. The power of love and compassion will conquer all.

We also have the idea that the practices of forcing practice changes on others hasn't worked in over two and a half millennia, so we need to consider that beliefs don't need to be changed. We need to be okay with not being right and not being exactly like someone else. Many have told me that they are embarrassed for believing in a practice as long as they did, and I remind them they should never be ashamed. There were lessons to be learned to get them to where they are today. We have absolutely no say in someone else's interpretation of their deity relationship, nor the spiritual sources they may be communicating with.

Embrace your uniqueness. Know that there has never been, nor will there ever be, another person like you. You are incredibly unique and offer your distinctive perspective on a relationship with a deity and spiritual entities. No one will ever see things the same way you do, except for your interpretation of your deity figures. This is perfectly normal and completely acceptable.

One of the most powerful messages is the message from mother earth. In my beliefs, I have applied the name Freyja to her. She represents the sacred feminine aspects of our eternal existence. As we seek to come back to our birthright beliefs of spirituality, we need to seek to help the earth and protect the sacred. Being one with the earth provides our physical selves with many benefits, but the energy that Freyja offers us is unconditional and the limitless power of love.

Being religious doesn't make anyone more right than anyone else, and just because other beliefs don't agree, it doesn't mean they have all the answers either. We each have a journey to complete that includes the interactivity with both our spiritual beings and our deities. Our journeys are unique and should be an intimate exchange between us and our spiritual sources.

At the end-of-the-day, the spiritual entities we interact with and our deities want us to experience a lifetime filled with love, compassion for one another, and harmony with the earth. They have never directed, nor appreciated the direction of our journey by those shameful practices of division, hate, and dictation of our beliefs. While there has always existed the opportunity for deceit and societal status enhancement, those who came before us saw it for what it was: a damaged ego. We must be sure that we accept those interpretations with open arms.

Choices

We all have choices. We have choices during each second of our lives as to how we want to proceed. We have choices that affect the immediate and other choices that affect our long-term growth. Spirituality moves differently for everyone, and each may have their own interpretations of the messages they receive from their spiritual connections. We need to respect one another's individual quest for their connection to their spiritual entities and learn to only offer our experiences. Do not expect others to alter their beliefs to match ours. We have a choice to extend our unconditional love to everyone, whether inhabiting a physical body or not. We must be intentional about loving each other.

Giving others the same privilege of making their spiritual choices aligns with the assignment of love. By allowing others to make the choice to follow their heart, we begin to understand the expression of unconditional love toward our fellow human being.

Embracing Our Connections

As we consider our spiritual connection to the magical properties of this plane of existence, we must keep in mind each level of this connection between ourselves and our spiritual surroundings. We must seriously contemplate mindful activities to allow ourselves the opportunity to receive those connections from extrinsic forces and dedicate some thought as to how to use the information received to better ourselves, our family, and our clan. With this is mind, let's remind ourselves about our interactivity with each of the levels.

We have now learned that our spiritual self communicates with the spiritual realm through our aura. This interface requires us to have a clear frame of mind in which to request or receive information from our spiritual entities. We can manage several key factors that further allow our aura to be successful in connecting to the spiritual realm.

1. Our beliefs in the spirits and deities;
2. Our mental state, especially the emotional control we have;
3. Our intention, as we know that intention based on love and compassion is far more powerful than the others.

In addition, hopefully I have introduced you to the spiritual sources around us that can help us succeed. As a reminder, you have:

- Interactions with the spirits of other physical beings. This level creates the social fiber of the clan, or community we live in. This interconnectivity between members of a community demonstrates a sharing of love with others. By embracing community members within our aura of love and compassion, our journey to empathy is underway.
- Interactions with our spiritual ancestors afford us the opportunity to receive knowledge and wisdom about our emotional experiences

and struggles. With a history of encountering the same emotional challenges we have, our ancestors provide guidance of methods to navigate our situations. This wisdom should be sought to help align our paths to an ancestor's emotional journey.

- Interactivity with the spirits of the lands, or the Landvætti, connects each of us to the expansive wisdom and knowledge of what will ever be known, as the Landvætti have inherited this level of knowledge from the deities in the beginning. We should seek this wisdom or knowledge when pressed against an unknown. By actively seeking the wisdom, we create a vacuum within the spiritual realm to attract spiritual entities to assist us.

- Interactivity with our interpretation of the deities. Deities possess the universal energy of creation. Many interpret this energy as the power of love. Deities are the only entity in all the levels of existence that create something from absolutely nothing. Some translate the earth itself as a deity entity, explaining how life is passed to the physical plane, thereby creating something from nothing.

Our Lifetime of Love

Through this text, I have referred to an idea of emotional control that allows us to experience empathy. While many of us simply absorb the dictionary definition of what empathy is, there is so much more. Primarily, empathy is the ultimate expression of love. It shows that we are willing to look past our own needs to that of another, to feel their pain. This is love, my friends. While we may not always see the same path, and we often see life from different perspectives, love binds us all. Love is a gift from the deities of the deities, and as mentioned in the emotional control chapter, it possesses the universal energy of a deity.

Love does conquer all. It provides light to the dark, warmth to the chill, comfort to the pain, peace to the chaos, and harmony to those who embrace it for what it really is. Love is energy. Love literally binds us together. It is the driving force that bonds a spiritual entity to our physical self for a lifetime of learning the prize of emotional intellect.

Mother Earth loves each of us, every day. She does it without concern for what most of us do to her every day. While she simply waits for each of us to return to her without our physical bodies, she maintains an eternal sense of hope.

She sends her love on the fragrant scent of the blooming flowers, or the morning dew upon the grasses, even the gentle breeze on a hot day.

She hopes that each of us will help her recover from the sickness of greed and ego centricity. Hope that each of us comes to know what and who she is.

If we ponder the definition of love and consider its implications in our everyday life, we know that we are capable of many expressions of love.

- Empathy is love. It is the embrace of loving someone other than our selves strongly enough to feel their emotional struggles.
- Sharing is caring, and caring is love. It is love of another person to offer them whatever we have to fill a vacuum in their life.
- Teaching is love. Caring enough about another's misunderstanding to teach them.
- Acceptance is love. Caring enough about another's beliefs to accept them just the way they are.
- Forgiveness is love. Putting aside emotional memories to let the darkness be illuminated in a relationship is love.

There are so many ways in our everyday life that we can choose to express love and come together as the humans we are destined to be. Our love should be central to everything we do and are. Choosing to express our love toward the physical beings on this plane is something we can intentionally do. This is one of the strongest powers within the universe, and it is natural for the physical existence, as it is the energy that Mother Earth gives us.

Many have wondered (myself included) how to demonstrate our love for others. This is a complicated question. Ultimately, the idea of demonstrating our love is to put other's needs above our own, to open our hearts to embrace the emotional connection through another's aura. Because of the emotional connections we have made within the different parts of the brain, many may interpret love differently.

I'll use my personal life as an example. My beautiful bride has intrinsic needs for physical contact and concentrated time spent together. In my mentality (until recently), I have always viewed love as my needs being satisfied. Whether it be intimate relations, or meals, or whatever. This is where I failed to identify what she needed as a demonstration of my affection for her. Now mind you, we have been married for 30+ years, and one might say that after raising five children and assisting with three grandchildren, our life has become routine. Mundane, if you will. However, this does not change the fact that as my beautiful bride continued her genetic/chemical modifications, her needs may have changed. As her husband, I should take the time to recognize that her needs should supersede my needs to spend time on my phone catching up with emails. So, understanding her position means that I put down my phone and provide some concentrated time and physical contact, as this is her interpretation of someone loving her.

Our definitions change because our genetic changes occur throughout our lifetimes. When two parties are in a relationship, we must listen with our hearts to what the other party needs and recognizes as the expression of love. This is the dynamic to love.

However, as I've mentioned, when love is placed central in our hearts, we find that the actions (needed from my example) occur naturally. Using the same example, during the earliest days of our relationship, although infused with lust, my attention to her needs of concentrated time and physical touch was abundant. Therefore, while her needs haven't changed a lot, my understanding of what her needs were and why she needed them did.

Love is the energy we feel from Freyja (Mother Earth) every minute of every day. This is the energy that should encourage us to love all who come into our sphere. We should use traits like:

- Empathy
- Sympathy
- Sharing
- Friendship
- Warm welcomes
- Acceptance of differences.

All these are vessels for us to transport our love to others. They are the public demonstrations, as well as the intrinsic values included in love. Remember, love is energy. It is a very powerful energy, and by sharing the love with others, not only do you bring in this energy to the self, but you pass it on to all the others you share it with.

Exercises

The exercises here are simply the same exercises that I use to investigate things that seem to cause an increase in tension and/or stress in my life. When these events occur, I note who I was with and what was said that triggered an emotional response. I use the final two exercises each day to ensure I keep my spiritual connections as open as possible to allow for the clarity of thought to pass through to me.

Let us perform a short exercise.

To complete this exercise, we will ask ourselves a series of questions. Just as important as our honest answer is noting how we feel about the answer. Our emotional interaction with the answers is how we listen with our heart. We will need to explore our deepest thoughts and feelings about what we think we believe. First, let's try an exercise just to get the connection strings functioning and see how things work before getting to the next section.

Let's set the stage. Get a notebook and pencil and find a comfortable place to be seated where we won't be disrupted. Once seated comfortably, close your eyes and slow your breathing just a bit. Deep breaths. In and out. Deliberate. With your eyes closed, picture in your mind the canyon walls of Utah or Arizona. Majestic and awe-inspiring. Fresh mountain air, just after a shower with a hint of the water sources. Relax. Feel the tension melting away.

As we begin our inventory, after asking the question, contemplate deeply how you feel. Make note of the feelings you have. Do not be discouraged if it takes several sessions and maybe different places to start feeling things. I find that my experiences have better results when I am outside, in contact with the earth herself. By having less urban interference and more of nature's spirituality, I am more apt to feel things a little stronger than otherwise.

Intrinsic Belief Inventory

Statement #1: "I believe in one god, and I call him/her _____." Seriously think about how you feel about this. Remember, we're listening for our feelings about this. If your heart seems a little negative or apathetic about this statement, you can follow it with "I believe in many gods". Again, note your feelings. You may want to include a statement about no gods at all as well, as your personal theism may be more animistic in nature. While we note our feelings on each of these statements, we want to seriously think about them. Focus on the question. Our personal theology should not only feel right and comfortable, but it should make sense in our mind. It needs to make sense in our finite mind as to how this deity, or deities, came to be, and what their function in relation to us is. If you are a practicing Christian, for example, you may want to follow up with more questions about individual parts of the doctrine, such as "I believe in Jesus" and so on. Again, if it feels comfortable saying it and thinking it, then it's probably right for you.

Statement #2: "I feel comfortable with what I understand from my talks with my god(s)." This begins to explore the idea of where we are in our spiritual walk, as it uncovers our desires to have an intimate relation with our deity. On the other side of that coin, if we question this, then I suspect we remain at the practice level of our religious understanding. We might want to utilize time to explore our individual relationship with our deity and come to know him/her/them more personally. This section of our learning may seem more uncomfortable because of the millennia of training we've inadvertently received saying that this type of behavior exhibits mental instability or is evil in nature. Nothing could be further from the truth. Without an intimate relationship with your deity, most will struggle to have healthy relationships with other physical beings as well.

Statement #3: "My relationship with my deity is different than any other relationship, and therefore I don't expect others to have the same relationship with their deity." This statement should incite something, as it seems to be one of the strongest carry-overs from those early practices. Whether others have multiple deities or no deities should have no effect on our relationship with our deity(s), nor should it affect our relationship with that physical being. The concept of converting others or seeing them as evil because they believe something different is a method of control. What many people don't understand is that the control being exerted is not against those we are attempting to convert, but on ourselves to see this as an important part of our beliefs or allowing this to alter our relationship with others.

Statement #4: "His/her belief in something totally different is completely acceptable." This continues the discussion as to where you are personally with your walk with your deity and spirituality. Being secure enough in our relationship with our deity so we are not offended by other's beliefs is a wonderful place to be.

After obtaining the results to the many questions, we can begin to construct our core theology. Don't worry when it doesn't match the mainstream teachings. Your theology can change throughout your lifetime. One of the other notes here would be to add other names instead of your deity. For example, if you are a practicing Muslim, you may want to try saying "I believe my god to be Zeus." Again, note the response your heart gives. Just so you are aware, most of those emotion hormones mentioned earlier are released near the heart, so your responses received could be extreme or not. The idea is that we are listening (or feeling) for an emotional response to these questions.

Eradicating Emotional Charges

Exercise 1. Be forewarned, you may discover emotional charges during this or similar exercises that may be quite painful to remember. The key is to power through it to regain control of your emotional state. In the same way as outlined in the previous chapter, the first task is to locate somewhere you can relax without being disturbed. Sometimes that might be out in the car in your driveway; however, the closer you can get to nature, the better. Having those spiritual entities support us can be super helpful and can provide a wealth of universal energy to tap into.

I recommend you either sit comfortably or lie on your back, as this allows for the greatest opportunity to relax all the muscles of the body. Close your eyes. Focus on your breathing. Breathe in and out. Slowly. Deliberately. Big breath in, let it out. Focus on listening to yourself breathe. Feel the tensions flowing away as your body relaxes completely, feel your extremities sagging as your tensions escape. All your weight should be along your back and/or bottom. You should be very comfortable now. Your breathing is slow and rhythmic. Your body is totally relaxed.

Now, picture in your mind a small, clear puddle of water. You can see the mud below the surface of the water. Think of this as your mind. Your mind is a clear puddle that you can see through. Think of any thought you have that might be in that puddle. Anything. Politics or medical science or nature. Anything. Be deliberate in your thoughts; pick a particular situation, or thing, and focus on it for a minute. When we focus on one thought, our brains connect us to other things that may be related. Allow your mind to wander through the images in your mind. Make note of anything that causes concern or uncertainty, certainly if we feel anger or upset. Those are the thoughts that we want to focus on. Why do we believe this? Why do I have this reaction to this? What am I supposed to learn? Why haven't I forgotten about this by now? We want emotional involvement, as this indicates that there are emotional issues surrounding this memory.

This exercise may take many attempts to slowly identify and address those small emotional charges tucked away in your mind. I would recommend about 15 – 45 minutes per day of taking time to clear the mind. Focus on the clear little pool of water. See the ripples from the wind brush across its surface. This little pool of water has helped me refocus my mind in the hurried busy-ness of my day.

More Exercises to Consider

In consideration for additional clarity of transmission between the spiritual realm and ourselves, we need to continue asking our brain those questions to ultimately become content with what we know and how we feel about what we know. The importance of clearing all these memory charges cannot be overstated. By having better control of one's mental state, one can expect more clarity from their spiritual interaction.

- Why am I struggling to understand?
- Casting out Judgment
- What do we believe spiritually?
- Finding our new theology

Once we get through our understandings of what we believe, then we can start asking questions about other beliefs. These questions are not meant to question the legitimacy of other practices but are an attempt to investigate if there might be an ancestral calling for us. Once we find the understandings that make sense and feel right, other questions allow us to better understand other's interpretations of their spirituality and bring us closer in our spiritual understandings. This is the goal. This outcome will help us to remove the many methods of division and separation that have existed for millennia.

Bibliography

While I did not use any direct quotes from any of these sources, I encourage all who read my book to please select these for additional reading. My knowledge was given to me by the Landvætti, but my encouragement came from these works. Although my interpretation is a little different, these works can help you find inner peace as you discover your spirituality.

Beck, Peggy V, Walters Anna Lee, and Francisco, Nia (1977) *The Sacred: Ways of Knowledge, Sources of Life.* Tsaile, AZ: Navajo Community College Press. pp. 95-136, 165-198.

Kvilhaug, Maria (2020) *The Seed of Yggdrasill.* Georgia: The Three Little Sisters. pp. 77-192.

Konstantinos (2002) *Nocturnal Witchcraft: Magick after Dark.* Woodbury, MN: Llewellyn Publications. pp. 37-56, 93-108, 181-190

Blamires, Steve (1995) *Magic of the Celtic Otherworld: Irish History, Love & Rituals.* Woodbury, MN: Llewellyn Publications. pp. 3-12, 61-80, 165-198, 291302

Millar, Angel (2021) *The Path of the Warrior Mystic: Being a man in an age of Chaos.* Rochester, VT: Inner Traditions. pp. 95-124, 152-160

Owen, Sarah (2021) *Celtic Spirituality: A Beginning Guide.* Las Vegas, NV: Unknown Publisher. pp. 16-65

Weatherup, Katie (2019) *Practical Shamanism: A Guide for Walk in Both Worlds.* USA: A Hands over Heart Publishing. pp. 17-36, 46-55, 122-134.

Flowers, Stephen E. Ph.D. (2005) *The Galdrabók: An Icelandic Book of Magic.* Smithville, TX: Rûna-Raven Press. pp. 24-59

Eggertsson, Jochum Magnús (2015) *Sorcerer's Screed: The Icelandic Book of Magic Spells.* Iceland: The Icelandic Magic Company. pp. 23-173

Ruiz, Don Jose (2018) *The Wisdom of the Shamans: What the ancient masters can teach us about love and life.* San Antonio, TX: Hierophant Publishing. pp. 1-46, 89-110, 131-170

Ruiz, Don Jose (2020) *The Medicine Bag: Shamanic rituals & ceremonies for personal transformation.* San Antonio, TX: Hierophant Publishing. pp. 1-40, 73-96, 173-214

Custers, René et al. "*Genetic Alterations That Do or Do Not Occur Naturally; Consequences for Genome Edited Organisms in the Context of Regulatory Oversight.*" Frontiers in bioengineering and biotechnology vol. 6 213. 16 Jan. 2019, doi:10.3389/fbioe.2018.00213

Kaldera, Raven, Krasskova, Galina (2012) *Neolithic Shamanism: Spirit Work in the Norse Tradition.* Rochester, VT: Destiny Books. pp. 1-24, 318-324.

Snellgrove, Wayne William (2019) *Daily Medicine: 366 Days of Spiritual Meditations.* Yorktown, VA: Blue Fortune Enterprises LLC.

Snellgrove, Wayne William (2021) *Whispers from the Hollow Bone.* Yorktown, VA: Blue Fortune Enterprises LLC.

ACKNOWLEDGEMENTS

I would like to thank my beautiful bride who has taught me so much throughout our more than 32 years of marriage. Without her, I would have never arrived where I am today, as she helped me to truly experience the chemical reaction called Love.

My mother, who initiated my journey of understanding of the cosmos for what it is and was not ashamed of being outside what everyone else thought.

I'd also like to give a shout-out to "Grobber" of the Tucson chapter of the Hells Angels Motorcycle Club®, who's interdiction saved my life and set me on the path of redemption and recovery that I can only hope to repay after this physical life… Ride free, my dearest friend… you will never be forgotten…

I'd like to send a giant "Ahéhee`" to the ancestral spirit of John "White Sands" Kettle, whose understanding of the Navajo spiritual beliefs added concrete to what I understood prior to spending years in his tutorage in Tucson, Arizona those many moons ago… Fly free my teacher…

I'd also like to thank Dr. Don Ashley for another launching pad during a theology undergraduate course at Wayland Baptist University here in Anchorage, helping me understand the separation between the theology and the religion.

I'd be terribly remiss if I didn't thank all my wonderful kids, who put up with me, regardless of how crazy I may have sounded sometimes.

Finally, I'd like to thank "Astrid," who truly taught me to fly.

ABOUT THE AUTHOR

Dr. Mark-Nathaniel Weisman is a Celtic/Norse shaman who lives in the land of the midnight sun of Alaska with his wife and two of their five children. A grandfather of four, he spends most of his time interacting with returning veterans helping to combat their symptoms of post-traumatic stress disorder in addition to being a shaman to a substantial following who seek an understanding of spirituality. His mannerisms and easygoing personality have made him a favorite among the many groups he interacts with. A third generation Dane born in the United States, he embraces his rich cultural practices while living in a technological world. Mark enjoys the beauty of Alaska from the saddle of his Harley Davidson motorcycle when not on the ice playing hockey.

A former monotheistic minister, Dr. Weisman's deep study of many spiritual doctrines around the world have provided him with his unique spirituality, which he has been able to share with others. As a staunch supporter of peace, harmony and cooperation, Dr. Weisman brings a wealth of understanding to the most powerful energy in existence: Love.

You can find Dr. Mark-Nathaniel Weisman at his website, akulfhednar.com or on Facebook at Alaska Ulfhednar. To reach him directly, email shaman@akulfhednar.com.

www.ingramcontent.com/pod-product-compliance
Lightning Source LLC
Chambersburg PA
CBHW072006110526
44592CB00012B/1223